UNDERSTANDING SUICIDE

A Case Study Approach

UNDERSTANDING SUICIDE

A Case Study Approach

by

DAVID LESTER

NOVA SCIENCE PUBLISHERS, INC.

Art Director: Christopher Concannon
Graphics: Elenor Kallberg and Maria Ester Hawrys
Book Production: Michael Lyons, Roseann Pena,
Casey Pfalzer, June Martino,
Tammy Sauter, and Michelle Lalo
Circulation: Irene Kwartiroff, Annette Hellinger,
and Benjamin Fung

Library of Congress Cataloging-in-Publication Data

Lester, David, 1942-
Understanding suicide : a case study approach / by David Lester.
p. cm.
Includes bibliographical references and index.
ISBN 1-56072-149-9 : $59.00
1. Suicide--Case studies. 2. Suicide--Prevention--Case Studies.
I. Title.
HV6545.L429 1993 93-30930
362.2'8--dc20 CIP

6080 Jericho Turnpike, Suite 207
Commack, New York 11725
Tele. 516-499-3103 Fax 516-499-3146
E Mail Novasci1@aol.com

Printed in the United States of America

Contents

Preface

The aim of this book is to introduce the reader to current thinking about suicide. What do we know about the causes of this serious problem, and what kinds of questions can experts answer?

In order to illustrate the topics and issues raised in this book, I have included a number of case studies. The suicides of famous people have aroused great interest and stimulated many biographies. I have chosen to use case studies of famous suicides because their lives have been described and dissected in much greater detail than have the lives of ordinary people who have taken their own lives. Thus, we have a wealth of information for most of the cases presented here, and I have been able to present only a brief summary of each case. If you are interested, you can of course find much more information on the people both in the sources I have used and in other biograhies that have appeared on them.

I was tempted to cut the case studies in length so that each would illustrate the particular point that I wished to illustrate with the case, childhood loss in Marilyn Monroe or psychiatric illness in Virginia Woolf, for example. I decided instead to include reasonably full accounts of each case so that you can endeavor to make sense of the suicide using all of the available information without having recourse to the original biographies.

I kept the case studies in full also because, even though I have been researching suicidal behavior for many years, I still feel that I have little understanding of why people kill themselves. I first became interested in the case studies included in this book because I hoped that by reading of an Ernest Hemingway or a Marilyn Monroe, I might come to a better understanding of at least why one person committed suicide. For some of the cases presented here, I do feel that suicide makes sense for them, that it flows from the course of their life and was, in some way, inevitable and even fitting.

Perhaps you, the reader, will also come to such an understanding?

CHAPTER 1

Defining Suicide

At first sight, it may seem foolish to devote a chapter to the problem of defining suicide. Suicide is said to have occurred when a person kills himself or herself. Isn't it that simple?

Let us examine whether this definition is satisfactory. First let us consider how we know that someone has completed suicide. (Completed suicide is the term we use to indicate that someone has died as a result of their suicidal action. Attempted suicide refers to those who attempt suicide but survive the attempt.) Typically we rely on a death certificate signed by a physician, often after an investigation by the police and the medical examiner.

Many investigators have claimed that deaths are often misclassified. On the whole, suicidal deaths are "hidden" by being misclassified mainly as accidental or undetermined deaths. Indeed Douglas (1967) suggested that selective undercounting of suicides by misclassification could account for differences in the reported suicide rates in different social groups.

For example, the heavily Roman Catholic nations of Ireland and Spain have very low reported suicide rates, as do Islamic countries such as Saudi Arabia and Egypt. Might not these low rates be due in part to the fact that suicide is considered a sin in the major religions of those countries and that those responsible for classifying deaths cover up suicides so as to permit the deceased to be accorded the customary funeral rights and to spare the family of the deceased suffering from the stigma of having their loved one labeled as a suicide?

It was common after Douglas's book appeared to claim that national suicide rates were invalid and could not be used by researchers. However, in the following year, Sainsbury and Barraclough (1968) looked at the suicide rates of immigrant groups in the USA and found that the relative ranking of the groups matched the suicide rates of their home nations almost exactly. Irish immigrants to the USA, for example, had higher suicide rates than the Irish in Ireland (a phenomenon that is true for almost all immigrant groups), but the Irish immigrants still had one of the lowest suicide rates of all immigrant groups, even though now their deaths were being certified by American medical examiners. As a result, the researchers breathed more easily. Although official suicide rates may be underestimates, there may not be too much systematic bias involved in which the suicide rates of some groups are heavily under-reported while those of other groups are less under-reported.

Nonetheless, there is good evidence that suicides are under-reported. Apart from anecdotal reports of medical examiners who will not classify a death as suicide unless there is a suicide note (and since only about 35 percent of suicides leave notes, this would

Dorothy refused. She loved life in New York and felt that her in-laws disliked her for having a Jewish father. She soon moved out to her own apartment. (Eddie permitted Dorothy to divorce him in Connecticut for cruelty in 1926 and to retain his name.)

Dorothy was fired early in 1920 from *Vanity Fair*, and the two Roberts (Benchley and Sherwood) resigned in protest. They soon got other jobs, but Dorothy remained unemployed. She also seemed to have stopped writing. (It always seemed to others that writing was a distasteful chore for Dorothy.) Nothing appeared in 1920 or 1921. But in 1922 she fell in love again.

Unfortunately, she fell in love with Charles MacArthur, a young newspaperman and a womanizer. But now her writing could proceed again. Her pieces appeared in the leading magazines, and she and friends wrote a revue (*No, Siree!*) that ran for a month.

As her relationship with Charles began to ebb, she discovered she was pregnant. She had an abortion, and soon after attempted suicide. She was home in her apartment and asked for food to be sent up. When the waiter arrived, he found her in the bathroom with her wrists slashed. Some of her friends thought she intended this as a gesture; others thought it was a sign of her disorganization and impulsiveness. After this, she began to drink more.

At thirty, Dorothy was still beautiful. She was also neither married, divorced, nor celibate. She lived in a cheap apartment building, with no close female friends. (Later in life, she would be close to Beatrice Ames and a few other women.) She was witty and a good writer, but in 1924 she hardly wrote.

By 1925 she was writing the poems that would be in her first book *Enough Rope*, some sweet and poignant, others flippant and ironic. But she also attempted suicide again, this time more seriously. Robert Benchley and others found her in her apartment, comatose from an overdose of drugs.

One of her stanzas from this period is:

If wild my breast and sore my pride, I bask in dreams of suicide;
If cool my heart and high my head, I think, "How lucky are the dead!"

Her next lover was Seward Collins, heir to a national chain of tobacco shops, a patron of the arts who adored her. In 1926 they went to France to meet the American intellectuals in Paris, ending up with the Murphy's on the French Riviera. Dorothy and Seward quarreled during the trip, and Seward left for America. Dorothy stayed on till October, arriving home with a best selling book - of poems no less. Soon she was an enormous success, contributing to *The New Yorker* and *The Bookman*, well-publicized and talked-about.

Dorothy began to tire a little of her group. It seemed trivial; it lacked any meaning. She began to get involved with political issues, supporting Sacco and Vanzetti, anarchists accused of murdering during a payroll robbery. They were executed on her thirty-fourth birthday. In 1928, her second book of poems was published, and she was involved with a businessman, John Garrett.

But she was beginning to write the short stories on which her claim to literary stature would be based. "Big Blonde" won the national O. Henry Prize as the best short story in 1929.

She next had an affair with John McClain, a clerk on Wall Street, had an appendectomy for which, despite her income, she couldn't pay. (Dorothy always had to rely on her friends to manage her life.) She pursued gaiety and drank heavily. (She even went to Alcoholics Anonymous for one meeting, and her biographer, Keats, considers Dorothy to have been an alcoholic in the modern sense of the word.)

Life With Alan

In 1932, Dorothy met Alan Campbell. In 1933 she married him. He was twenty-nine and she was forty. Alan was also half Jewish and half Scottish. Alan was a minor actor, aware that his talents were meager. He had hopes of taking Dorothy to Hollywood where they could work together on movie scripts.

Life with Alan soon fell into a pattern. They had fun but quarreled a lot. They even got divorced for one period but remarried. They worked well together on scripts. Between 1933 and 1938, they received screen credits for fifteen films, including "A Star Is Born" and earned lots of money that they quickly spent. They drank heavily, and Dorothy put on weight.

Alan liked Hollywood, but Dorothy did not. This led to frequent sojourns to New York, followed by trips back to Hollywood. For a while they owned a house in Bucks County, near Philadelphia (where she miscarried after three months of pregnancy), and commuted across the country to Hollywood.

Although Dorothy said that she was happy during this time, Keats describes her as ".....living with a fretful husband in a rather oddly furnished house, quarreling with her friends, allowing herself to grow dumpy in barren middle age, wasting her time on silly scripts, stunning herself with alcohol and sleeping pills....."

Dorothy took up the anti-Nazi cause in the Spanish Civil War, even calling herself a communist. She went to Spain in 1937 to view the war from the Loyalist side. (The result, of course, was the blacklisting of both her and Alan in the 1940s, and even more so in the 1950s during America's hysterical anti-communist witch-hunt.)

Alan joined the Air Force, and Dorothy was both proud of him and scared of him going off to war as Eddie had in the First World War. She followed Alan from camp to camp in America, as she had with Eddie, until he was sent to Europe. After victory, Alan stayed in London. Dorothy told friends he was involved in a homosexual affair. (She had accused him of homosexual leanings throughout their marriage.) And she divorced him. But this time, there were no suicide attempts.

Dorothy published nothing in 1945 and 1946. But after the divorce in 1947, she collaborated on a story, a play and a film script with her current lover (Ross Evans). In 1949, after being dumped by Ross, she called Alan who had returned to Hollywood, and they decided to get back together.

After they remarried in 1950, they lived in Hollywood, but they separated after two years, and Dorothy went back to New York, where she lived at the Volney Hotel with other lonely aging ladies. But three years later, Alan visited her in New York and persuaded her to return to Hollywood to work on a movie script with him. The movie was never produced, and that was the last script they ever worked on. They lived on their unemployment checks (of $300 a month each) until Dorothy was hired by *Esquire* to write book reviews for $750 a month. (*Esquire* continued to pay her this each month until she died, regardless of whether she sent them any reviews.[1])

After seven years in their small house in a seedy section of Los Angeles, Dorothy woke up one morning, to find Alan dead beside her. June 13, 1963. Dorothy was sixty-nine. She returned to New York, to the Volney Hotel where she stayed until she died.

Her last article appeared in the November 1964 issue of *Esquire*. She visited her old friend, Beatrice Ames, for dinners. Friends visited her but were often appalled by her drunken abuse and the squalor of the rooms. She eventually began to lose her sight. She died at the age of seventy-three on June 7, 1967, of a heart attack.

Her death merited an obituary on Page 1 and almost all of Page 38 of *The New York Times*.

Discussion

Dorothy's early adult life in Manhattan and her public reputation as a witty liberated woman obscured the other side of Dorothy. Her written work expressed the sadness over her life and her bitterness over the world, especially the lot of women. Despair lay behind most of her actions and writing. Her biographer describes her poems as ".....portraying a woman who said she was suspicious of joy, disillusioned as to love, contemptuous of and sorry for herself, and given to thoughts of death."

Later, after twenty-nine so-so years with Alan, Keats describes her as ".....crouched in silence, writing virtually nothing and drinking more than she ate, talking more to her poodle than with those who would be her friends, discontent with her present and dissatisfied with her memories of the past....."

Not a happy soul. Yet, she had a gritty determination to go on and could never quench her hope.

Her childhood was miserable; a mother dead early; a home with no love; a harsh father and an eccentric step-mother; and schools where she felt an outsider. (She made no friends from those years, and her family had no place in her life.)

Her two suicide attempts (some friends reported at least five) were in her late twenties and early thirties. Charles MacArthur had abandoned her and left her to have an abortion prior to her first suicidal gesture. Her second attempt two years later was more serious, but Keats gives no immediate precipitating cause.

What is more curious is that in later life, romantic loss and living alone did not lead to suicide attempts. Her classic poem on methods of suicide had concluded that "....you might as well live." And so she did. But why?

---

1. She did review 208 books for them, however.

Virginia Woolf

I have presented the suicide of Virginia Woolf in Chapter 4, an interesting person to compare with Dorothy Parker because they lived during the same time period and were both writers. They also were both centers of famous groups: for Dorothy the Algonquin group and for Virginia the Bloomsbury group.

The differences are immediately clear. Virginia had a much more stable home life, though she did lose her mother when she was thirteen. She married late in life, but had a stable and happy marriage (asexual though it might have been).

Virginia was much more of an intellectual than Dorothy. She wrote serious reviews of literature. She wrote novels that received critical acclaim rather than popular success. The Bloomsbury group discussed intellectual matters and was not simply a social group for witty repartee. Dorothy's was the life of those who ape the intellectuals; the theater, but not the symphony or the opera; drinking at speakeasies rather than gathering at friends' houses for talk.

With her husband, Virginia founded the Hogarth Press which published works such as those by Sigmund Freud. Dorothy and her husband wrote Hollywood scripts.

This is not to denigrate Dorothy. I have felt from my study of famous suicides that (some) intellectuals worry inordinately about issues that do not concern the rest of us. Some of them seemed to lack the capacity to enjoy life. Dorothy was not among those.

Dorothy's group reminded me of my immature years. I was part of a social group that tried to be humorous and witty.And I observed how such banter so easily turned hostile.[2] I found that being in such a social group engendered a cynical and hostile attitude toward the world, or nurtured the view that was already there. Since those early years, I have always avoided such groups.

But Dorothy was isolated from her family, without female friends, alone in New York. The Algonquin group was her only group.

Yet the most important difference between Virginia and Dorothy was that Virginia clearly had a bipolar affective disorder (manic-depressive disorder) from an early age whereas Dorothy seemed to be free from psychiatric disorder. The more disturbed of the two made the more serious suicidal act.

Marilyn Monroe

Although Marilyn Monroe (see Chapter 3) lived a generation after Dorothy, it is also interesting to compare her life with that of Dorothy.

Marilyn's childhood was much more disrupted than Dorothy's, though at each stop Marilyn probably had more friends and more affection than Dorothy had in her stable but awful home.

Like Dorothy, Marilyn's early suicide attempts were in response to loss of love. Like Dorothy, she drank heavily, but Marilyn abused prescription drugs more.

It is interesting to compare them in their thirties. Marilyn seems to be at the end of her career. She had been fired by the movie production company, she was divorced and

2. Americans in recent years have been fond of hostile humor, as illustrated by the success of comedians who ridicule others and by the "celebrity roasts" on television.

CASE 2: Joe Orton

Joe Orton was born on January 1st, 1933, as John Orton, in a lower class housing estate in Leicester. His mother Elsie, worked as a machinist until her eyesight failed and she had to become a cleaning lady. His father William worked as a gardener for the local government. Joe was their first child - he had a younger brother and two younger sisters. The family was quite poor. They had no telephone, no car, and no appliances. One of Elsie's treasures was a cheap pink Woolworth glass dish.

All the children remembered the home as unhappy. The parents bickered, and the home was drab and depressing. William had little to do with his children. Joe felt close to his mother, buying her birthday presents as a teenager, but not his father. (When he returned dutifully for his annual visit, he always brought Elsie gifts, but never lavished money on her as she expected. She died in 1966.) Elsie was often brutal to her children, beating them severely, on occasions until they were unconscious.

Elsie complained a lot about William, telling everyone she should never had married him. They never kissed, and once the fourth child was born, Elsie banished William to another room. After 1945, William never had sex with his wife.

Joe had asthma as a child and missed school a lot because of illness. He reported his first sexual encounter at the age of fourteen when a man masturbated him in a movie theater. But Joe was interested in girls for a while during his adolescent years.

Elsie believed that Joe had gifts, so after Joe had failed the eleven-plus exam for entrance to a grammar school, she decided to send him to a private school, not realizing it was a commercial school. Joe attended the school from 1945 to 1947. Teachers there remember Joe as semi-literate and poor at expressing himself in speech or in writing.

Somehow, though, Joe became interested in theater. He joined several local dramatic societies and was thrilled at any part he was given. He decided to try to enter the Royal Academy of Dramatic Art (RADA) and took elocution lessons to improve his diction and prepare for the examination. He even took jobs to try to save money for the tuition should he be accepted. However, he hated the low level jobs he got, and he was usually fired. Theater gave him his only success.

Joe auditioned at RADA in January, 1951 and was accepted. The Leicester government helped out with the tuition. An attack of appendicitis delayed his arrival until May, 1951. It was there that he met Ken.

Kenneth Halliwell

Ken's father, Charles, was a chartered accountant. The family lived in a neat duplex near Liverpool. Ken was born on June 23, 1926, and his mother, Daisy, was told it would be too dangerous to have any more children. Ken grew up shy, keeping to himself. He read a lot and liked dressing up and acting. He developed into a mother's boy, always clinging to his mother when company was around. She pampered Ken and was close to him.

In September, 1937, Daisy was stung by a wasp and choked to death in front of Ken. Ken and his father were left together, but the relationship was cold and distant. His father ignored him, and Ken ran away from home many times.

Ken became interested in the theater and joined the local dramatic society in which he was very successful, much more so than Joe later. Although he went to grammar school, Ken stubbornly refused to go to University. From 1942 to 1951, he played prominent roles in twenty productions. In 1944, Ken became a conscientious objector, refusing to fight in the war, and served in the coal mines at Wigan, Lancashire.

In 1949, Ken's father committed suicide by putting his head in the gas oven. Ken was twenty-three years old. He came downstairs, saw his father, stepped over the body and turned the gas off. After having his morning tea and a shave, he went next door to the neighbors to call the police.

He auditioned at RADA at the same time as Joe, but was rejected. Finally, he persuaded RADA to admit him, and he paid for his own tuition from the small sum of money his father had left him.

Life With Ken

Joe soon moved in with Ken, and they became lovers. In their two years at RADA, surprisingly, Joe did well and Ken poorly. Ken was inhibited and wooden on stage, far too anxious. Joe graduated while Ken received only a Certificate of Merit. Joe worked for a few months as an assistant stage manager but disliked the work. His contract was not renewed. Ken went off to work on the stage for a summer season in Wales, his only work as an actor.

They came back to London and lived together again. Writing was Ken's idea. Together they wrote several novels. Initially, Ken wrote and Joe typed. Gradually, Joe played a more important role, until their works were truly joint efforts. Because they had only Ken's inheritance to live on, they lived an ascetic life. They wrote during the day to limit the electric bill. For three years, they both worked for six months each year at a factory to earn enough to buy a new apartment. A publisher recalls a meal served by Ken of rice with sardines followed by rice with syrup.

Joe worked hard at developing his skills. He practiced with lists of words, sentences, word constructions. They began to submit their work in 1955, but it was regularly rejected. However, Charles Montieth at Faber & Faber saw potential and encouraged them. He took them out to dinner and gave a party for them.

In 1957, Joe and Ken began also to write their own individual works, which also met with rejection. In 1958, Joe "invented" a character he called Mrs. Edna Welthorpe who wrote letters to the newspapers and to companies. In these letters, Joe again was practicing his literary skills and expressing his hostility. (In one of his first letters from Edna, she requested permission to use the local Baptist Church Hall for a performance of a play on homosexuals called *The Pansy*.) Joe's last novel, *Head To Toe*, was written in 1961 and published only after Joe's death.

In 1959, they started taking books from the public library, pasting in pictures incongruent with the content, writing obscene descriptions of the books and generally defacing them. The changes were funny, but they were also obscene and hostile.

In 1962, Joe and Ken were arrested for this defacing of library books. They were sentenced to six months in prison, sentences they served in separate prisons. Ken was repentant after the prison time, but the experience seem to have given Joe a focus for his writing and a new level of skill for his writing.

Ken was a failure in his career. He was a bad actor and did not graduate from RADA. He could not get his writing published or sell his paintings. For most of his adult life, Ken was sustained by his close relationship with Joe. Although Joe was incredibly promiscuous, always on the lookout for a casual sexual encounter, these other sexual experiences were only casual. Ken remained his only lover.

However, as Joe's success grew, Ken was faced with the contrast between Joe's fame and his own failure. Sensitized by the earlier loss of his mother (and his father), Ken could not face losing Joe. The murder-suicide served to escape from the unbearable pain of his life and to destroy the person he had come to hate.

Joe was a successful comic playwright. But as a human being he seems to have been thoroughly obnoxious. He was alienated from his family. He had few friends, though many acquaintances. He was involved in a long-term relationship with Ken, but continually cruised through the public toilets of London and the beaches of Morocco for casual sex. He was involved, admittedly, with a very neurotic individual in Ken, but Joe does not seem to have the interpersonal skills to build a good relationship.

Joe was a self-centered, angry and vulgar person. But what is of interest here is the possibility that he played a role in precipitating his own murder. Was Joe committing suicide by getting someone to kill him?

Ken had threatened suicide many times to Joe, and so Joe knew that Ken was in a state of despair. Joe had refused to have sex with Ken for years, and Joe's sexual indifference to Ken was contrasted by his strong sexual appetite for strangers. Not only this, but Joe documented all of this in his diary which he knew Ken read. In the last few weeks of their life, Ken had in fact physically attacked Joe.

In this situation, it would be reasonable to fear for your life. You would take care not to antagonize the other person, and you would try to get out of the situation quickly and carefully. Not Joe.

To some extent, therefore, it seems reasonable to conclude that Joe played a role in precipitating his own murder and that this may have been motivated in part by, possibly unconscious, suicidal motives.

Unconscious Motives For Suicide

Kurt Goldstein (1940) believed that for a death to be suicide, the person must have a mature concept of death and must intentionally be seeking death in his suicidal actions. Since children probably do not have a mature concept of death (for example, they may believe that death is temporary, like sleep, and that the dead can come back to life), children cannot commit suicide.

Likewise, a hospitalized schizophrenic patient who hallucinates a voice telling him to run in front of a car, or a person on LSD who believes that he can fly and jumps off a building (to his unexpected death - unexpected to him) are not suicides since they did *not* intend to die.

Karl Menninger (1938), on the other hand, believed that the suicidal or self-destructive impulse could operate in covert and subtle ways. He saw the victim-precipitated suicides described above, for example, as being clearly motivated in part by conscious or unconscious suicidal impulses, as might the behavior of the child or the schizophrenic described in the previous paragraph.

In addition, Menninger saw chronically self-destructive life styles as suicidal. The alcoholic or drug addict, as well as the heavy smoker or grossly overweight person, are all hastening their death by their life style. Menninger called these behaviors *chronic suicide.*

Others destroy part of themselves. They may lose an arm or a leg in an "accident". They may blind themselves or castrate themselves intentionally, not unknown behaviors among severely disturbed psychotic psychiatric patients. In this case, the self-destruction is more adaptive than suicide, since the rest of the person, especially their mind, survives the destruction of part of their body. Menninger called such behaviors *focal suicide* since the suicidal impulse is focused upon one part of the body.

Perhaps the classic example of focal suicide is Oedipus, the mythical King of Thebes. He was abandoned by his parents because it had been foretold that he would kill his father and marry his mother. He was brought up by the King of Corinth and, when he heard the prophecy, fled Corinth to avoid fulfilling it. On the way to Thebes he argued with a stranger and killed him in a fight (his father). When he arrived at Thebes he helped the nation and was given the hand of the Queen in marriage as a reward (his mother). When he found out later that he had indeed fulfilled the prophecy, he went first to kill his wife/mother, but he found that she had already hung herself. He then took the brooches from her dress and tore his eyes out with them.

Can an Animal Commit Suicide?

This raises the issue of whether an animal can commit suicide. For Goldstein the answer would be an unequivocal "No." For Menninger the answer would be a definite "Why not?"

Schaefer (1967) argued that for an animal to commit suicide, we would have to show that members the species could tell life from death (or live animals from dead ones), that they could distinguish between a room in which animals would be killed and one in which they would be allowed to live, and finally that they would, under some circumstances, choose to enter the lethal room and be killed. With a mouse, he showed that it was perhaps possible to demonstrate the first two requirements. His mice did learn to distinguish between live and dead mice and between lethal and non-lethal rooms. (They refused to enter the lethal room.) He did not show that they would ever choose to enter the lethal room.

New Categories For Death

Shneidman (1968) examined the categories we use for classifying death (natural, accidental, suicide and homicide) and decided that they were inadequate. He asked why was it natural if a virus entered his body but homicide if a bullet entered. He saw little difference.

He suggested a new set of terms to classify death. *Cessation* was the stopping of the potential for any further experience. The life of our mind is over. *Termination* refers to the stopping of the physiological functioning of our body. People who are in irreversible coma have ceased but not terminated. Some cessations are temporary (for example, some of those coma patients do eventually recover consciousness), and Shneidman suggested *interruption* for this state of affairs. Finally, for completeness, he called the ongoing process of life and living *continuation*.

What about the role we play in our death? In *intentioned* behavior, we choose to kill ourselves in a particular way. In *subintentioned* behavior, we play a covert, indirect or unconscious role in our own death. In *unintentioned* behavior, we play no role in our own death. (And for attempted suicides who appear to be choosing to play a role in their death but who really are not, Shneidman suggested the term *contraintentioned* behavior.)

Although people were impressed by this proposal, the use of the words has not become widespread.

Conclusions

My intent in this chapter was to demonstrate that, though suicide may at first glance appear to be easily defined, there has been a great deal of discussion over what is and is not suicide and whether we accurately classify and count suicides.

Despite these ambiguities and debates, it must be borne in mind that suicide can be defined much more easily and accurately than a psychiatric diagnosis such as schizophrenia for which agreement between different psychiatrists viewing the same patient is quite low.

CHAPTER 2

Who Commits Suicide?

The Epidemiology of Suicide

Epidemiology is the study of the distribution of a disorder throughout the population. It answers the question of which groups in the population suffer most from the disorder. In this chapter we will examine the answer to this question and, in addition, explore some of the social conditions that are associated with particularly high or particularly low suicide rates.

Age, Race and Sex

Completed suicide is most common in the USA in elderly white males. Suicide rates are higher in males than in females, in whites than in blacks, and in those who are older. The following table shows suicide rates (expressed as per 100,000 per year) for the USA in 1980.

whites		blacks	
males	females	males	females
19.9	5.9	10.3	2.2

White males had the highest suicide rate. Whites had higher suicide rates than blacks, and males higher rates than females.

Let us look at the characteristics of the cases of suicide presented in this book, even though they are not a random or representative sample of suicides.

Bruce Clark	male	32	single
Judy Garland	female	47	married
Kenneth Halliwell	male	41	single
Ernest Hemingway	male	61	married
Leicester Hemingway	male	67	married
Paul Kammerer	male	46	separated
Yukio Mishima	male	45	married
Marilyn Monroe	female	36	divorced
Freddie Prinze	male	22	separated
Gabrielle Russier	female	29	divorced
Jody White	male	17	single
Virginia Woolf	female	59	married

you develop your intelligent abilities during your life prior to having children, your children may be high in intelligence because they inherit this acquired intelligence from you. Lamarckians could not propose any mechanism to account for the transmission of the acquired characteristics through the fertilization of eggs by the sperm, and so it was viewed as a superstition rather than a theory.

Of course, the power struggles have an extra layer of complexity, since the free world adopted the Darwinian idea while the Communists, newly in power in Russia, adopted the Lamarckian idea. (When he killed himself, Paul was packed, ready to go to Russia to pursue his research there.) And today, Christians in parts of the USA try to suppress Darwin's ideas in school textbooks because it conflicts with their ideas of the appearance of humans on earth, ideas based on the bible.

Darwin's ideas have clearly aroused intense emotions and conflicts between believers and nonbelievers.

Koestler tells us that Paul was, "....one of the most brilliant and unorthodox biologists of his time. He was forty-five when the joint pressures of an inhuman Establishment and his own all-too-human temperament drove him to suicide." Is this true?

Paul's Career

Paul was born on August 17, 1880, of Saxon ancestors who now lived in Austria. His family was prosperous, for his father, Karl, was the founder and co-proprietor of a factory for making optical instruments. After twenty years of marriage, Karl divorced his wife and married a Hungarian widow, Sophie. (It was her third marriage and she had two sons from previous marriages, while Karl had one.) Paul was born with three step-brothers, aged eighteen to twenty, who adored him.

In this setting, Paul developed into a bright child. His childhood seems uneventful, and he began by studying music at the Vienna Academy. He composed songs that were performed in Vienna and counted among his friends Bruno Walter, later a famous conductor, and Gustav Mahler, the composer.

Paul then switched to reading zoology at the University, and some biologists always held his interest in music against Paul. They saw him as a dilettante.

Paul had grown up with an interest in and an affinity for animals. His early articles were on reptiles and amphibians and published in naturalist journals. These articles were read by the eminent biologist Hans Przibram who was founding an Institute for Experimental Biology, which was a new branch of research, a break from the theoretical and descriptive zoology currently in vogue.

Paul began by organizing the aquaria and terraria and proved to be very successful in keeping the animals alive in these unnatural conditions. This point is of importance to the story because others could not replicate Paul's experiments to see if they would get the same results as he claimed because none of them could keep the animals alive in the laboratory. (Indeed, Koestler claims that no one had repeated Paul's experiments with proper care even by 1971.)

In 1909, Paul received a scientific prize for his research on salamanders. He also conducted research on the sea-squirt. Koestler argues that this research was much more pertinent to the Lamarckian hypothesis than the research that Paul conducted on the midwife toad. Yet it was this latter research that became the battle ground. The research in question was published between 1906 and 1919 in three major papers.

(Interestingly, Paul also gave general lectures on biology and on his research in particular which were very popular. These too were frowned upon by leading academics because it an unwritten rule that serious scientists do not seek popular fame.)

The Controversy

The battle over Paul's research was fought in England and published mainly in the scientific journal *Nature*. The major accuser was William Bateson. Interestingly, Bateson had started by believing in the Lamarckian hypothesis. But after a fruitless expedition to Central Asia to search for confirmation, he switched to believing Darwinism. (Bateson named his son after the Russian geneticist Gregor Mendel, whose work contributed an important element to Darwinian theory.)

Bateson visited Vienna in 1910. He already thought that Paul's work was fraudulent, and his belief was confirmed when Paul could not produce specimens of the midwife toad to show the acquired characteristics. (Koestler explains that these characteristics, pads on the forearms of the toad, appear only in the mating season, and Bateson was not in Vienna during the toads' mating season.)

The problem of verifying Paul's work was made complicated by the First World War, which led to the destruction of many of the specimens in the Institute. Most of the animals died during this period. Paul himself was excused from military service because of a heart condition, but was assigned to censoring the letters from Italian prisoners and so could not continue his research. Following the war, the inflation in Austria led to the ruin of many, including Przibram and Kammerer. The Biological Institute was taken over by the Austrian Academy of Science.

All that remained to show skeptics were some slides and specimens preserved in jars. In 1920, the Institute sent Bateson some slides of the pads on the midwife toad, but he regarded them too as frauds, probably cut from a different species of toad. Once Bateson had made up his mind, Koestler argues, nothing would change it.

In 1923 Paul was invited to visit England to lecture on his research. He did so and brought with him a preserved specimen of the midwife toad showing the pads. Interestingly, Bateson did not attend the first lecture, but did attend the second. At the second lecture he did not examine the specimen. Koestler puzzles over this. Bateson, firmly believing that Kammerer has faked his research, refused to examine the evidence. Is this a true scientist? Clearly not. For Bateson, Darwinism had become a religion, and research is irrelevant to religion.

However, after Paul had returned to Vienna, Bateson wrote requesting that the specimen be sent to him for examination! The Institute refused, for it was the sole remaining specimen and Bateson had declined to view it four months earlier. Bateson saw this refusal as proof of the fraud.

Paul resigned from his post at the Institute in order to support his family by journalism and lecturing. He went twice to the USA for lecture tours (in the Fall of 1923 and the Spring of 1924). One unfortunate consequence of his lectures in England and the USA was that the newspapers wrote up his ideas sensationally. Headlines read *Race Of Supermen* in London and *Scientist Tells Of Success Where Darwin Met Failure* in New

Luxembourg	16.5
Malta	00.0
Martinique	11.9
Mauritius	03.9
Mexico	01.7
Montserrat	00.0
Netherlands	10.2
Netherland Antilles	02.0
New Zealand	10.2
Norway	12.4
Panama	02.0
Papua/New Guinea	00.2
Paraguay	02.7
Poland	12.7
Portugal	08.3
Puerto Rico	08.5
St Kitts & Nevis	00.8
St Lucia	00.8
St Vincent	00.9
Seychelles	03.1
Singapore	09.8
Spain	04.2
Sri Lanka	29.0
Suriname	14.2
Sweden	19.1
Switzerland	24.7
Syria	00.4
Thailand	07.1
United Kingdom:	
England & Wales	08.7
Northern Ireland	05.0
Scotland	09.9
USA	12.0
Venezuela	04.7
West Germany	21.4
Yugoslavia	14.8

However, these bare rates obscure the fact that suicide differs greatly in nature in the different countries in the world. To be sure, the ratio of men to women differs, as does the age distribution, and the methods used for suicide. But the motives for suicide vary also.

For example, Hendin (1964) compared suicide in the three Scandinavian countries and suggested that the differences in the rate and style of suicide were dependent upon the different ways in which the children were raised.

In Denmark, Hendin felt that people had learned to use their own misfortune to arouse guilt in others. Mothers use guilt arousal as a form of punishing their children. Danish people, including psychiatric patients, also have difficulty expressing aggression, a result of the fact that parents punish the expression of aggression in their children.

Danish children are encouraged to be very dependent, and this makes separation difficult for them to cope with in adulthood. Danish people are too egocentric to really care for others, and Danish men often have difficulty adjusting to the birth of their children. Suicide in Danes is often a result of loss and separation, and reunion fantasies are common.

Swedish people are very concerned with performance and success. The critical issue for Swedish men is their work. They are ambitious, and suicide typically follows a failure in performance. When they have difficulties at work, Swedish men avoid their wives and turn to male friends. Swedish mothers appear to shape this behavior by encouraging the child's early independence and rewarding self-sufficiency and success. The children often resent this pressure and respond with childhood phobias (a fear of the dark is common) and sleeping difficulties.

In Norway, where suicide is less common, the men develop a strong attachment to their mothers, combined with angry, tyrannical and dependent behavior. The impending death of their mother leads to a severe crisis. Norwegians seem to hold on to their anger, and life-long feuds are common. Depression is common in Norwegians, whereas Swedish men appear to be emotionally dead.

Unfortunately, this kind of provocative (though speculative) analysis has not been done for many nations.

In Japan, suicide is quite common as a result of academic pressures, which are much more intense than those in the USA, and as a result of thwarted love. However, there are forms of suicide in Japan that are rarely found in the USA. For example, suicide as an act of atonement is rare here, whereas hundreds of Japanese officials committed suicide when the Emperor was forced to surrender to the Americans, ending the Second World War. Suicide in the cause of one's country is not unknown in the USA, but the kamikaze pilots who aimed their planes at American ships and died in the wreckage astound us.

Yukio Mishima had some elements in his life that are found in American suicides. The close attachment to his grandmother (who relegated Mishima's mother to a very minor role) made her death when he was fourteen difficult to cope with. His concern with the decay and degeneration that comes with age is common in American suicides, though Mishima's concern focused upon his body rather than his mental capacities as in the case of Ernest Hemingway.

However, the Samurai tradition does not have its parallels here, and his ritual suicide by *seppuku* after failing to arouse the soldiers in support of the Emperor is very foreign to our culture.

His suicide resembles that of Paul Kammerer (Case 3) in the respect that each was trying to achieve something by his suicide, to die in such a way that a particular image would be created that might affect the society. Kammerer wanted to clear his name of the accusation of fraud, and Mishima wanted to stimulate a political movement.

They failed. Kammerer's suicide suggested that he was indeed guilty of fraud, and Mishima did not create a new movement in support of the Emperor. Yet they did change our image of them. And their lives are resurrected and dissected again in this book to help us understand suicide. Not what they intended for their memorials.

Here is Yukio Mishima's story. Can you understand the motivation of his suicide as easily as that of the American and European cases described elsewhere in this book?

School

Mishima entered middle school in 1937. His grades improved and, as his health improved, his attendance record became better. His teachers there also liked his writing better than had his elementary school teachers. Shizue encouraged her son's writing. Azusa had to work in Osaka for two years and, when he returned in 1939, was horrified by his son's interest in writing. He tore up a work Mishima was writing, and thereafter Mishima hid his writing from his father.

At the middle school, his literary ability led to his acceptance by the older boys and the inclusion of his work in every issue of the school magazine. His early writings already foretold his later mature works: irony and elegance, alienation from the lower classes and a delight in cruelty.

By fifteen, Mishima was still pale and puny and suffered from anemia, but his health had improved greatly since his childhood. He excelled at his schoolwork, and his writing ability facilitated his association with the older boys and with the teachers. (His parents used his ill health to get him excused from the mandatory two years of boarding at the school.)

From an early age, Mishima read European literature, and this influenced him greatly. Eventually, he would furnish his house in a European style, and visitors from the West found him to be the most accessible of the Japanese writers. (His teachers at his school did not forbid their students to read European literature even though the official militarist creed at the time was that the Japanese were superior to all other races.)

His mother signed Mishima up for instruction in writing outside of school also, in particular with the renowned poet Ryuko Kawaji. At age sixteen, Mishima published his first work in a literary magazine (edited by one of his teachers). It was at this time, in 1941, that Mishima chose the pen name he would use for his writing.

The War

The war brought little change in Mishima's life at first. Azusa was too old to be drafted. In 1942, he resigned from the civil service and started a law practice. Mishima's grandfather also died that year. Mishima moved up to the senior school, ranked second out of the sixty boys in his class.

Mishima associated with a group of writers who believed that the war was holy and that death in the service of the Emperor was the highest goal in life, especially since self-destruction would lead to reincarnation. This group of Japanese romanticists (the Roman-ha) had the official support of the military leaders.

Mishima passed his army medical in May 1944, and he was drafted into the local regiment for which he had to periodically work. In September 1944, he graduated at the top of his class and was awarded a gold watch by the Emperor personally.

CHAPTER 3

THE PREDISPOSITION TO SUICIDE

Surprisingly, suicide often runs in families, but it is far from clear why this is so. It might be the result of psychiatric illness running in the family, which itself might be due to a gene that is passed on from parent to child to grandchild, or because each generation teaches the next generation that suicide is an acceptable response to a crisis. However, before we discuss these possibilities in greater detail, let us look at a case in which suicide has occurred in at least three successive generations.

CASE 5: Leicester Hemingway

Ernest Hall was born in 1840 in Britain, came to the United States as a teenager and fought in the Civil War. Later, he made money in the cutlery business in Chicago. In 1905 he was dying and suffering from severe pain. He was planning to kill himself with a gun that he kept under his pillow. His son-in-law removed the bullets, and he tried to shoot himself with the unloaded gun.

His son-in-law was Ed Hemingway, a doctor. In 1928 Ed Hemingway suffered a financial loss from properties he had bought in Florida and in addition to this he discovered that he had diabetes which he had failed to diagnose and treat. He suffered from terrible headaches, hardening of the arteries and angina pectoris. He feared gangrene of his feet, a result of the untreated diabetes, which might have necessitated amputation. Ed Hemingway shot himself in his bedroom one lunchtime with a .32 Smith and Wesson revolver that had been used by his father, Anson Hemingway, in the Civil War.

Ed Hemingway had six children, including the writer Ernest Hemingway who committed suicide. His daughter, Ursula Hemingway Jepson, developed cancer and underwent three operations. She was depressed, and in 1966 she killed herself with an overdose of drugs.

Ed's son Leicester was born in 1915, in Oak Park, Illinois, and killed himself on September 13, 1982 in Miami Beach, Florida.

Leicester was the sixth of the six children, (Ernest was the second-born and first-born son.), Leicester was sixteen years younger than Ernest and did not get to know his older brother well until the 1930s. He spent much effort imitating and trying to win the favor of his older brother, but eventually (in the 1940s) Ernest rejected him.

Leicester (Hemingway, 1961) notes that he was unplanned. He was looked after by his five older siblings, and even Ernest sometimes changed his diapers . Leicester learned to hunt and fish from his father and Ernest.

Leicester remembers Ernest coming home from the First World War as a hero, and he remembers idolizing him. When Ernest later went to Paris with his new wife, Hadley, Leicester wrote to him to send him stamps and foreign money for his collection. Leicester went to Ernest's high school and wrote for the same school newspaper (*The Trapeze*). Ernest encouraged Leicester to be a writer and advised him to work in journalism as he himself had done.

Leicester was home in bed with flu on the day his father came home at lunch and shot himself. Leicester, only thirteen years old, discovered the body.

Leicester's features were similar to Ernest's, but he inherited his mother's blue eyes and blond hair. According to Meyers (1985), Ernest said that he always disliked Leicester because Leicester reminded him of his mother. He was also embarrassed by Leicester's enthusiasm and ineptitude and the failure of almost all his endeavors. He wrecked a boat he had built while sailing it to Cuba in 1934. He tried to be a sportsman, tough guy, and writer but never equaled Ernest. (Of course, had he ever equaled Ernest, Ernest would have been extremely jealous!) Ernest also felt that Leicester traded on Ernest's reputation and was a bore and a nuisance. When Leicester would write to his mother and tell her tales about himself that were false, Ernest would criticize him, ignoring the fact that he himself had done the same thing.

In 1936, Leicester married an adopted daughter of his Uncle Tyler, and they had two sons (Peter and Jake). He built boats, worked for the USIS in Bogota, went into the shrimp business, declared himself king of a tiny Caribbean island, was a bookmaker, a publicity man for a jai alai fronton in Miami, ran a charter boat in Montego Bay, and wrote adventure stories for a magazine in New York City. He published a war novel (*The Sound of Trumpets*) in 1953, which Ernest considered inferior. Later, Ernest burned one of Leicester's manuscripts without telling him.

Leicester spent time with his brother in Cuba during the 1930s, joining in his fishing and drinking adventures. Ernest needed to have a kid brother around, someone to whom he could show off, someone to teach, someone to admire him. Leicester himself noted that his worshipful awe of Ernest helped the relationship with his brother. For a while, Leicester filled the role of junior crony, obliging confidant and trusted playmate.

In a reversal of roles, it was Leicester in 1940 who took a small boat through the Caribbean searching for Nazi refueling stations for their submarines. Though Ernest never admitted it, he followed Leicester's example and spent part of the war searching for Nazi support groups in the Caribbean. Leicester worked in radio intelligence, a military film unit and the signal corps during the war and met up with Ernest in London. Leicester obtained frequent leaves either to assist Ernest or to nurse him through his injuries.

Leicester continued to imitate his brother after Ernest's death. He grew a beard and began to resemble him physically. For the last five years of his life, he published a small monthly newsletter on fishing (*The Bimini Out Islands News*), living with his second wife Doris and his two daughters (Ann and Hilary). He developed severe diabetes and had five operations. Threatened with loss of his limbs he became depressed. He shot himself in the head with a borrowed handgun (*New York Times*, September 15, 1982).

Analysis

Leciester's father shot himself, depressed and suffering from diabetes. Ernest shot himself, depressed and suffering from diabetes. Leicester shot himself, depressed and suffering from diabetes. Even if we grant the possibility of a genetic predisposition to depression, the modeling by Leicester of his life on the life of his revered older brother is noteworthy. Both suicides took place under similar circumstances, after a long life, and while suffering from a terminal illness, as did those of their father and sister.

Leicester's life seemed to be an imitation of his brother's, but much less successful in the view of commentators. Leicester was not considered to be as good a novelist or journalist. He was a mere side note in biographies of Ernest. The *New York Times* indexed his death under Ernest's name, and his suicide was seen as Leicester imitating Ernest once again.

The traumatic event in Leicester's childhood was finding his father's body after the suicide. A father whom he adored, came by to check on his fever and then walked along to his own bedroom to shoot himself. Much later, the brother whom he had worshipped shot himself. And in 1982, Leicester was suffering from diabetes and dreading the amputation of his feet. The illness would have restricted his life and prevented him from doing most of the things that gave him pleasure in life. The idea of suicide as a solution had been planted in his mind at an early age and, with the examples of his father and brother, it was the obvious thing to do.

◆ ◆ ◆

Is Suicide Inherited?

When we see families, like the Hemingways, in which people from several generations kill themselves, we often wonder whether suicide runs in families. Perhaps suicide can be inherited? And often the children of suicides come to believe that they will eventually kill themselves, as well just as children of parents who had heart attacks fear that they too will die from heart attacks.

The fact is, that many things run in families, including eye color, the sex of the children, physical and psychiatric illnesses, intelligence and careers. However, not all of these characteristics run in families because they are inherited. Eye color is an inherited characteristic, but your choice of career is not.

Parents pass on attitudes, opinions, desires, as well as genes to their children, and careful research is needed to weed out the characteristics that are inherited. Only two sound methods are commonly used to ascertain this. In cross-fostering, children whose biological parents have the target characteristic are adopted by parents who do not have this characteristic. The children are then followed up to see whether they resemble their biological parents or their adoptive parents. For example, in a study of babies born to schizophrenic mothers but adopted at birth by normal mothers, Heston (1966) found that these babies had higher rates of psychiatric disorder than adopted babies from normal mothers. No cross-fostering studies have yet been conducted for suicide. However, Schulsinger, et al. (1979) have found that adopted people who killed themselves had more suicides in their biological relatives than in their adoptive relatives.

The alternative technique is to find identical twins, separated at birth and raised by different families, and compare them with non-identical twins. If the identical twins resemble each other more than the non-identical twins, then genetic factors clearly play a role in this resemblance. No such studies have been conducted for suicide, but a weaker form of the research design has been used, in which identical twins and non-identical twins raised together have been compared. Since identical twins are treated more similarly than non-identical twins (Wilson, 1931), the greater resemblance of the identical twins could, in this weaker design, be attributable to genetic similarity or to the greater similarity in rearing.

The first data for identical and non-identical twins raised together was published by Kallman (1953) and further studies of small samples have been published recently. The overall concordance rate for suicide in these studies for identical twins, (that is, given that one twin has completed suicide, what percentage of the twin partners have also completed suicide), was 18 percent, whereas, for non-identical twins, the concordance rate was zero percent (Lester, 1986).

Thus, the data suggests that suicide may be inherited. However, there is strong evidence toward the inheritance of psychotic psychiatric disorders. For example, the concordance rate for affective disorder identical twins reared apart is 67 percent (Price, 1968) as compared to 14 percent for non-identical twins (Nurnberger and Gershon (1982). For schizophrenia, these percentages are 60 percent and 13 percent, respectively, (Gottesman and Shields, 1966; Slater, 1968). Thus, it is may be that identical twins could resemble each other in suicidal behavior because there is an even stronger similarity in the presence of psychosis. So far, research has not attempted to eliminate this possibility.

In the Hemingway family, Leicester killed himself with a gun, just as his grandfather had tried , as did his father and older brother, Ernest Hemingway. But there is also evidence that each of these men suffered from depression. Perhaps the similarity in suicide is a result of the inheritance of an affective psychosis? But, we cannot rule out the possibility of social learning. The Hemingway family may have learned that suicide is the preferred solution to depression and severe physical illness in old age. Children acquire all manner of habits and attitudes from their parents by observation and Leicester, a child of thirteen, was at home alone when his father shot himself. At this impressionable age, learning by observation may have occurred.

Physiological Causes

The 1980s have witnessed an explosion of research into physiological causes of psychiatric disorder, and some of this research has focused on suicide. Researchers have analyzed the urine, blood, cerebrospinal fluid and central nervous system tissue of suicides and comparison groups of people. Lester (1988a) has reviewed all of this research and found several clear conclusions. Suicidal involvement appears to be associated with abnormal responding in the response of cortisol levels in the blood after injections of dexamethasone, lowered levels of 5-hydroxyindoleacetic acid (one of the metabolic products resulting from the breakdown of serotonin), in the cerebral spinal fluid, a lower norepinephrine/ epinephrine ratio in the urine and possibly lower levels of serotonin in some areas of the central nervous system. Overall, the serotonergic neurotransmitter system seems more likely to be functioning abnormally in suicidal people than other neurotransmitter systems, and serotonin is the neurotransmitter that is the basis for the major biochemical theories of depression.

What this comes down to is that suicides have similar physiological characteristics to depressed psychiatric patients in general. Thus, all of this research has simply confirmed the finding that suicide is commonly and strongly associated with depression, an association we will examine more closely in Chapter 4.

Gender Differences in Suicide

One of the most consistent findings from research into suicidal behavior is that men kill themselves more than women, while women attempt suicide more than men. This sex difference has been found in almost all nations, all eras, and all subgroups of the population (for example, in white and black Americans and in all age groups).

For example, in a classic study in Los Angeles County, Farberow and Shneidman (1961) located 540 men but only 228 women who had completed suicide in 1957. In contrast, they located 1824 women but only 828 men who had attempted suicide. (Of course, many minor gestures at suicide were not counted because they did not come to the attention of doctors and other authorities. But even these mild gestures at suicide are typically made more often by women than more serious suicide attempts.)

Lester (1988b) has looked at the sex difference in completed suicide around the world. In 1980, the male/female suicide rate ratio ranged from 1.1 in Thailand to 9.0 in Guatemala. The ratio was 3.3 in the USA.

One obvious explanation for this sex difference in suicide is that women choose less lethal means of suicide, (such as sleeping pills and other medications), whereas men choose more lethal methods (such as firearms). For example, in Los Angeles in 1957, 19 percent of the men committing or attempting suicide used guns, as compared to only 3 percent of the women. In comparison, 53 percent of the women used barbiturates as compared to 26 percent of the men.

Let us look at the cases presented in this book.

Bruce Clark	gun
Kenneth Halliwell	overdose
Ernest Hemingway	gun
Leicester Hemingway	gun
Paul Kammerer	gun
Yukio Mishima	sword
Freddie Prinze	gun
Jody White	gun
Judy Garland	overdose
Marilyn Monroe	overdose
Gabrielle Russier	gas/overdose
Virginia Woolf	drowning

Even though this sample is not a random sample of suicides and cannot be considered representative of Americans in general, it is clear that the men used more lethal methods more often, while the women used less lethal methods. It has been argued that part of the reason behind women using the less lethal methods is because those methods are less disfiguring and their bodies look nicer after death (Lester, 1988c).

However, this difference in choice of suicide method is not a complete answer to the differences in sex, because Lester (1969) found that, *within* each method for suicide, men still died more than women, while the women survived more than men. Could women be physiologically stronger, allowing them to survive the trauma of their suicidal actions?

There is the possibility of physiological factors here as well. Attempted suicide in women has been clearly shown to vary over the menstrual cycle, and this variation may be a result of a changing psychological mood or changing levels of circulating hormones, (estrogen and progesterone). Attempts at suicide are more common during the premenstrual and bleeding phase of the cycle, and so the mood and hormone levels may create an excess of suicide attempts at these times? Interestingly, a recent report Vessey, et al. (1985) finds no differences in suicidal behavior among women taking birth control pills, (which also changes levels of circulating hormones), as compared to women using other methods for contraception.

Epidemiological studies of psychiatric disorder have shown that men typically have a higher incidence of psychosis, while women have a higher incidence of neurosis, (for example, Roth and Luton, 1943). Since completed suicide is more common in those suffering from psychosis, (see Chapter 4), this differential incidence of psychiatric disorder may also play a part in determining the sex difference in suicidal behavior.

Finally, Linehan (1973) found that the typical person in the USA views completed suicide as a masculine behavior and attempted suicide as a feminine behavior. When asked to predict the risk of completed suicide, people predicted a higher risk in men than women and a higher risk in masculine individuals than in feminine individuals. Linehan suggested that this perception of the behaviors may set up social expectations such as the fact that men view completed suicide as more acceptable while women view attempted suicide as more acceptable.

Several studies have reported higher rates of completed suicide, sometimes exceeding those in men, in professional women, especially in physicians, chemists and psychologists (Ross, 1973). A study in Canada, however, showed that working, married women had lower suicide rates than those who did not work (Cumming, et al., 1975). Thus, it is not working *per se* that is related to suicide, but rather working in a professional position.

Nations with greater female equality have lower rates of suicide in women (Stewart and Winter, 1977). Yet, the female suicide rate is rising in many nations (Gove, 1972). For example, in nine Western industrialized nations, the male suicide rate rose 2 percent from 1952 to 1962, while the female suicide rate rose 18 percent. The reasons for this difference remain unclear.

Childhood Experiences and Suicide

It is a common assumption in psychology that early experiences are critical in determining the course of our lives. Some of these experiences are well documented.

Parental Loss

It has long been known that depression is much more likely if a person experiences the loss of a parent during childhood. The same phenomenon is found in studies of suicides. In the 1970s, for example, thirteen studies found an excess of early loss in suicides as compared to comparison groups, while ten studies found no differences (Lester, 1983). Clearly, this phenomenon is not always found.

Some studies find that loss due to the death of a parent is more common in suicides, while other studies find that loss due to separation and divorce is more common. There seems to be no consistency in the research results on this point, though some reviewers of the research feel that loss due to separation and divorce is more critical for suicide (Phillips, 1979).

Research on the age at which the loss takes place and the sex of the lost parent seems to indicate no consistent findings. However, several studies have suggested that early loss combined with recent loss may be an especially potent factor in increasing the risk of suicide. Stein, et al. (1974) found a high incidence of early and recent loss in attempted suicides. Lester and Beck (1974) found that females who had attempted suicide and had experienced early childhood separation from their parents were more likely to have recent loss as a precipitant for their suicidal behavior.

These ideas are easily documented in the case of Marilyn Monroe. Indeed, the incidence of loss in the early years of Marilyn is incredible. Marilyn was shipped from foster family to foster family, even spending some time in an orphanage. In some of the homes she stayed, Marilyn grew close to the family and, when they moved away, leaving Marilyn behind, she must have mourned the loss. The psychiatric hospitalization of her mother when Marilyn was seven was also a severe loss, especially since they had recently grown a little closer.

In this context, it is interesting that Marilyn's first suicide attempt was after the death of her lover, Johnny Hyde. Although she had refused to marry him, she obviously loved him and, because he was much older than Marilyn, we can speculate that he combined the roles of lover and father for her. Marilyn's experience of early loss may have sensitized her to later loss, as Lester and Beck have hypothesized.

CASE 6: Marilyn Monroe

Biographers have reported very little about of Marilyn Monroe's paternal relatives, but her maternal grandparents were psychiatrically disturbed. Her grandmother, Della Hogan, was congenitally melancholic, and her grandfather was mentally unstable. Both died insane. Della was hospitalized at Norwalk State Hospital in August 1927, fourteen months after Marilyn's birth, and died there nineteen days later of a heart attack during a manic seizure.

Marilyn's mother, Gladys Monroe was born in 1900. Gladys was separated from her husband Martin Mortensen when she got pregnant by Stanley Gifford. Gifford's refusal to marry her or take care of her and the baby brought on a profound depression, the first of many in her life.

When Marilyn was seven, Gladys was hospitalized, eventually arriving at Norwalk State Hospital, like her own mother, Della. She remained hospitalized for most of her life and outlived Marilyn.

Perhaps Marilyn lived in fear of the defective genes that made her mother and grandmother mentally ill. Were those genes passed on to her and would they also lead her to end her days in a mental hospital?

(Marilyn believed that her Uncle Marion killed himself, but Marion's daughter said that he simply deserted his family.)

Marilyn's Childhood

Gladys decided not to take care of her baby, whom she named Norma Jeane. Instead, Marilyn was boarded with a family, the Bolenders, across the street from her grandmother. Gladys visited Marilyn regularly on weekends and took care of her intensively once when she got whooping cough. The Bolenders were fundamentalists and very strict. Marilyn was beaten with a strap for misbehavior. They had an adopted son, Lester, and the two were quite close. Marilyn used to call Mr. Bolender her father.

At this point in her life, Marilyn seems to have been a lively, curious and adventurous child. The major loss was when her dog, Tippy, was run over.

When Marilyn was seven, Gladys decided to take over the care of her daughter. She bought a house, rented it to a British couple and then rented back a couple of rooms for herself and Marilyn. Marilyn's life became much freer now. She was able to indulge in her love of movies, and went to them whenever she could. She also fantasized about her missing father a great deal.

After Marilyn had been living with her mother for just over six months, Gladys was hospitalized for depression. (She was taken away while Marilyn was at school.) Marilyn stayed with the British couple for about a year and then, after they left the country, with neighbors, the Giffens. Gladys had a friend, Grace McKee, named as Marilyn's guardian and refused to let the Giffens, (who already had three children), adopt Marilyn. When the Giffens moved, Marilyn, now eleven, went to the Los Angeles Orphans' Home Society, where she stayed for twenty one months. Her guardian, Grace, visited her regularly there.

Eventually, Grace married Doc Goddard and rescued Marilyn from the orphanage. However, she placed Marilyn in two foster homes briefly before bringing her home early in 1938. In this home, Marilyn had three other children for companionship and became friendly with one, Beebe, who was two years younger than Marilyn.

Here, Marilyn also became close to Grace's Aunt Ana, a widow, and to whom she remained close until Ana's death ten years later. Ana introduced Marilyn to Christian Science.

The Goddards were neighbors to the Doughertys who had a son, Jim, about five years older than Marilyn. The stories about the development of the relationship between Jim and Marilyn conflict. Certainly, Jim picked Marilyn and Beebe up after school and drove them home. He took Marilyn to the high school dance. Certainly the Goddards planned to move to West Virginia, and Gladys would not let her daughter go with them. At this time, Marilyn was living with Aunt Ana who perhaps noticed the seductive ways of the young Marilyn and thought it a good idea to get her safely married.

However it was arranged, Jim and Marilyn married on June 19, 1942. Marilyn was sixteen and Jim was twenty-one. And there is evidence that they loved each other sincerely and had a good marriage for the first few years.

These first sixteen years have several noteworthy features. Clearly, Marilyn's life was unpredictable. Who would keep her? And for how long? Would she be put in a orphanage? Would her mother take care of her? Or would Gladys go crazy and leave her?

Then, who was her father and where was he? How much loss would she suffer? First the Bolenders left, then her mother, the British couple, the Giffens, and now the Goddards. As soon as you got close to someone, they up and left. Even her dog was run over.

Was she loved? Was she liked? If she was liked and loved, maybe her father wouldn't have disappeared, maybe one of those families would have kept her, and maybe she wouldn't have to had to go into the orphanage.

The two factors most critical for a child are to have a safe and predictable world and to be loved and liked for yourself. Marilyn had neither. But at least she now had a loving husband.

The First Marriage: Transition Years

Marilyn's marriage to Jim Dougherty was reasonably happy. For the first couple of years Jim worked and, since he didn't want Marilyn to work, she stayed home. Marilyn was happy and came to enjoy making love. However, she still found the attention of other men rewarding, and this would make Jim jealous. Eventually Jim decided he wanted to join the service, but Marilyn was distraught over this. He joined the Merchant Marine as a compromise and, as his initial posting was to Catalina, they lived together. But then Jim asked to be shipped overseas. His first tour kept him away for one year. Marilyn was faithful during this leave.

His first leave was wonderful. Interestingly, just before Jim was due back, Marilyn called her father (Gifford) who hung up on her. Jim's second departure was more upsetting than his first, and Marilyn moved from staying with her in-laws to staying with Aunt Ana. During the two years he was away, Marilyn wrote him about two hundred letters. (Yet years later, she claimed it was marriage of convenience!)

After his first tour, she began work in a factory, and in 1945 an Army photographer, David Conover, noticed her in the plant and encouraged her to begin a career as a model, with Aunt Ana's encouragement. By the time Jim returned from his second tour, Marilyn was busy with her career as a model and had disengaged from Jim sexually and emotionally. He refused to leave the service, and she refused to stop her modeling career.

This episode is interesting. Jim must have known that he would lose his attractive and flirtatious wife if he went off to sea. Yet he went. Marilyn was abandoned by her first love and lover. She was described as distraught by his first departure and even more by his second. The loss must have recapitulated all of the other losses and leave-takings she had experienced as a child.

One wonders. If he hadn't left, if he had encouraged her career, would her life course have been similar to the one we know?

Marilyn's Career

Marilyn was successful as a model and set out to break into movies. She began by divorcing Jim in Nevada, (in May 1946), since movie studios did not like married women. She started with Twentieth Century Fox, (where she chose the name Marilyn Monroe), and began the stress of trying to build a career in movies.

She was cut by Twentieth Century Fox after two six-month contracts and by Columbia after one. She, like others, called her agent all the time, hoping for a part or an engagement, dealing with the disappointments of having nothing to do or getting only minor assignments. She was poor. In 1948 she fell in love with Freddie Karger, but he would not marry her. However, she did remain close to him and his family. In that year Aunt Ana died. Marilyn lost an important mother figure, but found another in Natasha Lytess, the head drama coach at Columbia. Marilyn lived with Natasha for a while and developed her acting skills with Natasha's guidance.

Marilyn was taken over by Johnny Hyde, a good agent, who devoted the last few years of his life to establishing Marilyn's career. Marilyn moved from Natasha's to Johnny's house and become his lover. He wanted to marry her, but she told him that, though she loved him, she was not in love with him.

By the time he died in 1950, Johnny had persuaded Twentieth Century Fox to give Marilyn a seven-year contract, and she had two good roles (in *The Asphalt Jungle* and *All About Eve*). However, when he died, his family ordered her out of his house, and she went back to Natasha's. She was very depressed and took thirty Nembutal tablets, but was discovered and rescued by Natasha.

Johnny represented Hollywood. Twentieth Century Fox wanted Marilyn to be a sexual object in movies. Natasha saw greater acting ability and wanted Marilyn to search for better roles. Yet Marilyn doubted her ability. Marilyn continually took lessons to improve her skills, with Natasha, with Lotte Goslar to learn mime, and with Michael Chekhov and Lee Strasberg to improve her acting. Yet she needed her coach with her all the time, especially on the movie set. First Natasha and then Paula Strasberg accompanied her all the time, continually coaching and reassuring her.

In 1950, Marilyn had plastic surgery on her nose and chin. (She had previously used a retainer to pull in her front teeth a little and had switched from dirty to light blonde.)

By the end of 1951, Marilyn was becoming well known. She had met and become attracted to Arthur Miller, (who was married and lived on the East Coast). Again, she tracked down her father and tried to visit him, and again he refused. In 1951, Marilyn's tardiness began to become a problem. She became increasingly concerned about her looks and would take two hours or more in front of her dressing room mirror trying to perfect her appearance before coming out. Natasha had destroyed Marilyn's trust by financially tricking her on two occasions, but Marilyn continued to be dependent upon her presence as a coach.

In 1952, Marilyn met Joe DiMaggio. They had little in common and had a stormy relationship. She was doubtful about marrying him, but finally did so in January 1954. The marriage was over by September 1954. He opposed her career, objected to her public sexuality, and was violent on occasion. But nonetheless, she was very upset at the breakup.

However, Marilyn remained committed to her career. If marriage to Jim, and now to Joe, meant that she would have to leave her career, then marriage was out. Her career would go on. She started an independent company (Marilyn Monroe Productions) to purchase and produce films for her.

By the end of 1954, Marilyn had made other changes in addition to her break with Joe. Natasha was replaced by Paula Strasberg as her coach on location. She decided to leave Hollywood and move to New York City, (which facilitated her relationship with Arthur Miller), began to study with Lee Strasberg and entered psychoanalysis with Marianne Kris.

She was also well established as a star (appearing in *The Seven Year Itch*), and becoming much more assertive about the films she made. Her new contract with Twentieth Century Fox greatly increased her pay and gave her control over the choice of directors.

She moved back to Hollywood, living with Milton Greene and his wife. (Milton Greene was her business partner in Marilyn Monroe Productions). Miller divorced his wife in 1956 and married Marilyn.

Marriage to Miller and the Decline

Soon after her marriage to Arthur Miller, Marilyn and Miller went to Great Britain to make a film directed by Lawrence Olivier. Miller was in conflict with Milton Greene, (Marilyn's business partner), and Paula Strasberg, (her coach). He wrote critical things about Marilyn in his journal, which she found. After Marilyn read Miller's comments on her, she was distraught, and her psychoanalyst flew over from New York to help calm her down. Marilyn had severe conflicts with Olivier, but the film was made.

In the years of marriage to Miller, Marilyn had two miscarriages and made several suicide attempts. The first was in the autumn of 1957 with barbiturates, while Miller was at home. He got medical assistance for her.

She made two movies (*Some Like It Hot* and *Let's Make Love*), but she was becoming increasingly difficult to direct in movies. She was anxious about being on camera and angry with people connected with the movie. She was often late to the set and temperamental as are many stars. However, in 1959 she received minor awards for acting, (from France and Italy), and performed with the classes at Lee Strasberg's Acting Studio. But by 1960, Miller had virtually stopped writing and was spending his time trying to keep Marilyn together.

During the making of *Let's Make Love*, Marilyn had an affair with her co-star Yves Montand. For much of the time Miller and Simone Signoret (Montand's wife) were away, giving Marilyn and Montand freedom. When Miller eventually flew back to Los Angeles, it was clear that the marriage was over. But Marilyn and Miller agreed to stay together while his screenplay, *The Misfits*, was filmed with Marilyn in the lead.

During the shooting of the movie, Marilyn was taking uppers (Benzedrine) and downers (Nembutal). She spent sleepless nights, screaming at Miller, or drugged. Her lateness on the set continued. At one point, she was flown to Los Angeles under the supervision of her psychiatrist Ralph Greenson to withdraw from Nembutal and switch to a milder drug.

As soon as the movie was finished, Miller moved out of Marilyn's Los Angeles house, and they disentangled their possessions in New York and Connecticut as well. Clark Gable, Marilyn's co-star in *The Misfits,* died soon after the shooting was over, and his wife blamed his heart attack on the stress of working with Marilyn.

Back in New York, Marilyn was emotionally and physically ill. She tried to persuade herself to jump out of the window of her apartment, (but failed), and her analyst in New York hospitalized her in the Payne Whitney Clinic. The clinic horrified Marilyn, especially her status as a suicide risk and the presence of other disturbed patients. She eventually managed to call Joe DiMaggio who checked her out and moved her to Columbia Presbyterian Hospital.

Back in Los Angeles in 1961, she began to rely on her psychoanalyst there, Ralph Greenson. Greenson invited Marilyn to come and live with his family, but when she declined, he had a friend of his, Eunice Murray, become her housekeeper. In May and June she had minor surgery, (to remove her gall bladder and part of her pancreas). She was befriended by the "Rat Pack", a group including Frank Sinatra and Peter Lawford, and they moved Marilyn into the social life of the Kennedy's. She had an affair with John Kennedy but later became involved with and very attached to Robert Kennedy.

In 1962, she bought a small house, similar in style to Greenson's and moved in. She continued to visit New York, (where she saw her New York psychoanalyst and John Kennedy). In April shooting began on *Something's Got To Give*, and Marilyn became Robert Kennedy's lover. However, her inability to work on the set led to her being fired by Twentieth Century Fox.

In July, Marilyn had an abortion and was very depressed. She began to see Greenson daily. In July, Robert Kennedy began to disengage himself from his relationship with her.

Marilyn killed herself early on Sunday morning, August 5th, with an overdose of Nembutal and chloryal hydrate. On Saturday night, Greenson had visited her and Eunice Murray had stayed over. Robert Kennedy was visiting San Francisco with his family that weekend.

There is speculation that Robert Kennedy visited her that Saturday, that the Kennedys had Marilyn killed and that the Mafia had her killed. But perhaps it doesn't matter what really happened in her final weekend. Marilyn was disintegrating rapidly. It is hard to imagine that she could have survived much longer.

ANALYSIS

Marilyn's Genetic Inheritance

The mental illness in Marilyn's mother and maternal grandparents suggests that Marilyn may have had an affective psychiatric illness with a genetic basis. Of course, the existence of psychiatrically disturbed parents does not prove a genetic cause for the disturbance. Crazy parents create a disturbed childhood experience for their children, as well as passing on their genes.

However, Gladys seems to have done both. The childhood she created for Marilyn was the worst possible kind for someone with a genetic predisposition to depression.

What is especially noteworthy is that Marilyn lived with the fear that she would end up disturbed like her mother and grandmother. So the fear of becoming crazy may have been as potent a factor in her eventual disintegration as the actual genes that she may have inherited.

Marilyn's Disturbance

Interestingly, Marilyn appears to have few psychiatric symptoms in her early years. Only a mild stutter and painful menstrual periods are noted. In adulthood, there is evidence of headaches, excessive alcohol intake and drug abuse, (especially uppers and downers). There is a history of depressive episodes, most of them occurring soon after the loss of a love or lover, and attempts at suicide. (Interestingly, the two attempts documented in detail by Guiles both occurred with someone close at hand.) There are three psychiatric hospitalizations, one for drug abuse and two for depression.

Back in the 1950s and 1960s, there were few good psychiatric treatments for depression. Antidepressants were not readily available, and Marilyn was spared electroconvulsive therapy. Marilyn's depression remained untreated. (We do not know what type of psychotherapy was conducted by her analysts Kris and Greenson and whether it was appropriate.)

Mother and Father Figures

Marilyn had two major types of figures in her social network. To substitute for the mother she never had, Marilyn usually had a close relationship with a female, usually a coach or mentor, first Natasha Lytess and then Paula Strasberg. In childhood, there were a succession of mother figures, but only Aunt Ana seemed to have provided the basis for a good relationship, (in particular, with no rejection).

Marilyn's missing father seriously affected her life choices. Her two attempts to contact her father, rejected by him each time, only fueled her feeling of deprivation. She would look for and be attracted to father figures, and there were a succession of them in her life: from Johnny Hyde her agent to Arthur Miller. But men, especially confronted with a woman whose sexuality is so prominent, can hardly expected to fulfill the role of a father.

The Search for Approval

Because the little girl Marilyn was shuttled around from family to family and abandoned by most of them, Marilyn probably concluded that she was not very likable or lovable. Thus, she entered into the common pattern of suppressing her real self and adopting a false social self that would get her approval.

For Marilyn, who physically developed quite early and who was very pretty, sexuality was an easy choice. Aunt Ana noted the tight clothes and seductive behavior in Marilyn's early teens. After her first marriage at age sixteen, Marilyn still needed the attention of men. If men responded to her, then perhaps she was all right, a likable and lovable person.

Unfortunately, if you attract the attention of men, you also stimulate their sexual desires. So many of the men eventually became her lovers. Toward the end of her life, especially with the Kennedys, we have to wonder whether John or Robert really cared about Marilyn. By then, she was disintegrating, chronically depressed and taking drugs heavily. Their relationship with her must have been based primarily upon her fame and availability for sexual intercourse.

Not only, therefore, would the men in her life disappoint her, by abusing her and abandoning her, but they would not provide the unconditional love that she needed then and had needed even more urgently as a child.

Therefore, Marilyn adopted, the tactic of getting attention by her looks and sexual style. Her tardiness may have been caused in part by her depression and drug abuse, but it was also a result of her insecurity (will people really like *me*?) and her reliance on her looks for attention.

She had her teeth straightened and minor plastic surgery and took incredible care getting ready for public appearances. Marilyn's looks had to be perfect because the little girl she once was, the real Marilyn, was far from perfect as proved by all of those adults who abandoned her.

Marilyn's Emotional States

We have discussed Marilyn's depression and hinted at her insecurities. In all likelihood, she soon developed a fear of abandonment and the loss of love. She attempted suicide after losing Johnny Hyde and killed herself when Robert Kennedy was about to discard her. She could never trust people, and unfortunately her life experiences appeared to prove that she was right to distrust others.

Socially, she often appeared to be shy, especially in groups. She had a fear of meeting strangers. (Perhaps they would see her inadequacies?) And her directors and co-stars were aware of her insecurities as an actress. (It is interesting that she never appeared in a play on stage. She performed in only one or two scenes from plays at the Actor's Studio.)

There appears to have been strong inner anger that led to angry outbursts and displays of bad temper. At the end of her marriage with Arthur Miller, she spent nights awake screaming curses at him.

Clearly this inner anger stemmed from the anger at her mother and father for abandoning her. Every betrayal and desertion thereafter would feed into this anger, and it would be felt toward the new rejecting person and also renewed toward her parents.

Distorting the Past

One habit of Marilyn is of particular interest because she shares it with Ernest Hemingway who also killed himself. Marilyn distorted the past.

She claimed that her dog was killed by a neighbor. (It was run over accidentally). She claimed horrible mistreatments at the orphanage that appear to be false. When she was young she claimed that Clark Gable was her father. She was smothered by her grandmother (but at an age when she could hardly have remembered) and raped by a boarder, (except that she never lived with anyone who took in boarders).

Like Hemingway, Marilyn moved on, abandoning old friends and locales. And like him she distorted the past, making it usually worse than it was. Is it that she wanted to arouse sympathy? Or that she thought that Marilyn's real life was boring and needed embellishing?

Intelligence

Marilyn is described as being intelligent, but she was poorly educated, leaving school at sixteen. She seemed to have been bothered by this. She tried to read good literature, but Miller noted that she dipped into books and rarely finished them. She was shaky about the names of the authors and their characters.

Her lack of education may have added to her doubts about her worth. Having decided, (consciously or unconsciously), to get attention by means of her looks and sexuality, perhaps she feared being seen as a dumb blonde. Yet, her intellect was not developed.

Related to this, she had never received training as an actor. Here, however, she was willing to take classes, though she would become over-dependent upon her coach because of her self-doubt over her acting ability.

Social Resources

It is worth noting that Marilyn usually lived with or was very close to families, most of which gave her affection. (The list includes the Bollenders, Goddards, Doughertys, Kargers, DiMaggios, Greenes, Strasbergs, Millers, and Greensons.) She always had friends and affection.

But none of these families and friends was enough. Because none of them could take the place of mom and dad.

Final Stresses

At the end of her life, Marilyn had lost her job. She had been fired from a movie for the first time. She was about to lose her current lover, Robert Kennedy. Her addiction to drugs was greater than ever and her depression as bad. She had analysts in Los Angeles and New York to respond to her needs daily. (She seems to have been terrified to be without a therapist close at hand.)

What was in store for her? The decline of her fame as a movie star. Abandonment by her lovers. And aging was making it more difficult to appear in public as beautiful as she once thought she was. Marilyn was nothing but a beautiful women on screen and an attractive sexual object in bed. Age changes that.

Like Hemingway, Marilyn was close to the end of her life as she defined it, just as Ernest was at the end of his life as he defined it. Both, in fact, had arrived at an existential choice point. To create a new existence or to end the old one. Both chose to end the old one.

◆ ◆ ◆

If we look at the experience of loss in our cases, we find a high incidence and a common age.

Bruce Clark	father died/age 2
Judy Garland	father died/age 13
Kenneth Halliwell	mother died/age 11
Ernest Hemingway	no early loss
Leicester Hemingway	father committed suicide/age 13
Paul Kammerer	no early loss
Yukio Mishima	grandmother died/age 14
Marilyn Monroe	break up of foster home/age 7
Freddie Prinze	uncle & grandmother died/age 14
Gabrielle Russier	no early loss
Jody White	father committed suicide/age 14
Virginia Woolf	mother died/age 13

The incidence of loss is high (75 percent), and the most common age for the loss is not in the first few years of life, but rather in late childhood at the age of 4 to 14.

Although the loss of family members by suicide is not common, suicides do appear to have a higher incidence of experience of loss through suicide. In a recent review of the research on this issue, Lester (1987a) found six studies reporting an excess of suicides in the families, relatives and friends of suicidal people and eight studies which found no differences. These studies, therefore, appear to indicate an excess, (albeit a modest excess), of suicidal behavior in the significant others of suicidal people. Kreitman, et al. (1969) has also documented an excess of suicide in the social networks of suicidal people and noted that this was especially true for those less than thirty-five years of age.

There is also a growing body of research on the experience of abuse and later suicidal behavior, and occasional studies do find an association. For example, Green (1978) found a higher incidence of self-mutilation and suicidal behavior in abused children as compared to neglected and normal children.

Psychiatric Illness in Parents

Several studies have reported an excess of psychiatric illness in the families of suicidal people, though the research is not consistent on this point. In suicidal teenagers, however, depression in the parents does appear to be more common (Pfeffer, et al., 1979). We can see in the case of Marilyn Monroe that depression and psychiatric illness was present in her mother and her grandmother, and Marilyn lived in fear that she too would have a psychiatric illness as they had.

Punishment Experiences

Virtually no research has been conducted on punishment experiences and later suicidal behavior, but punishment does play a prominent role in the theory of suicide proposed by Henry and Short (1954). Henry and Short argued that, when children are punished, they are frustrated and angry. If they are physically punished they are less likely to suppress this anger, for to express it results only in another slap. Thus children punished physically are likely to learn to express their anger outwardly and become assaultive (and in extreme cases murderous). On the other hand, if children are punished with the threat of loss of love, then to aggress against this frustrating parent makes the possibility of abandonment and loss of love more likely. Thus, these children are more likely to suppress their anger, eventually turning it inward, transforming it into depression and suicidal impulses.

In addition, punishment by the same parent who nurtures the child and provides love is more likely to force the child to inhibit the anger felt toward the parent when he or she punishes the child, for to express this anger may threaten the supply of love and nurturance. On the other hand, if one parent punishes the child while the other nurtures the child, the child is more likely to express his or her anger, for to aggress against the punishing parent does not threaten the supply of love from the nurturing parent. (In the traditional home, Daddy punishes, while Mother comes up to the bedroom to take care of the punished child.)

Since Marilyn had been moved from home to home during her early years, she may well have been afraid to express her anger outwardly for fear of being sent away to a new family or to an orphanage. Therefore, it is likely that she developed the pattern of suppressing her anger, and as a result, became depressed.

Although no direct research has examined the validity of these ideas in suicidal people, research supports the hypothesis in murderers. For example, Palmer (1960) found that murderers had suffered twice as much frustration from all types of sources as their non-murdering brothers. And Glueck and Glueck (1950) in their classic study of delinquents found that the delinquents were more likely to have been punished physically than non-delinquents.

Palmer presented the case of Mike who, at the age of eighteen, murdered a middle-aged prostitute whom he was trying to rob after having intercourse. Mike had been continually beaten as a child. When he was five, his uncle got angry with him and threw across the room so that he hit his head on a stove. His two older brothers once beat him with branches till he was covered in welts, after which he was ill for two days. On several occasions, his uncle put him under the hood of a car and started the engine. His uncle and brothers used to give him electric shocks just for fun. His brothers once threw him into a stream on the pretext of teaching him to swim and he nearly drowned. They had also tied a snake around his neck, causing him to "go out of his mind".

The Quality of the Parent-Child Relationship

The research that has been conducted on the nature of the parent-child relationship has been conducted primarily on suicidal teenagers since their parents are present and the relationship can be observed.

As you might expect, the quality of the parent-child in suicidal families is worse than in the families of less disturbed teenagers. For example, Korrella (1972) found that the parents of teenagers who had attempted suicide showed less affection toward their child. There was much hostility and resentment between the family members. Corder, et al. (1974) found poorer communication between family members with a suicidal teenager and stricter parental discipline.

However, research has not yet consistently identified specific features of families that produce a suicidal teenager as compared to families with disturbed, non-suicidal teenagers.

Jacobs (1971) has documented a pattern of chronic disruption in families of suicidal teenagers, in which parents go through multiple marriages and divorces. These parents and children were more alienated, and the parents were more likely to yell, nag and punish their children physically. The teenagers also showed more behavioral problems, such as running away from home. These families seem, therefore, chronically disorganized. Unfortunately, Jacobs compared his suicidal families with normal families, and so we cannot be sure that the features he identified are specific early experiences for suicide rather than for emotional and behavioral problems in general.

Sibling Position

Lester (1987b) has reviewed the research on whether suicidal people are more likely to be first-born or last-born. There appeared to evidence for an excess of first and middle-born in completed suicides and an excess of middle and last-born in attempted suicides. But research on much larger samples is needed before we can be sure about these conclusions.

What is the birth order of the cases in this book?

Bruce Clark	only (?)
Judy Garland	last born of 3
Kenneth Halliwell	only
Ernest Hemingway	2nd born of 6
Leicester Hemingway	last born of 6
Paul Kammerer	only in 2nd marriage
Yukio Mishima	first born of 3
Marilyn Monroe	only child
Freddie Prinze	only in 2nd marriage
Gabrielle Russier	no information
Jody White	last born of 3
Virginia Woolf	3rd of 4 in 2nd marriage

No clear pattern emerges from these data. There are five only children, one first born, two middle born and three last born but, without a comparison group, the apparent excess of only children cannot be checked.

Conclusions

In this chapter, we have reviewed some of the predisposing factors that may increase the likelihood of suicide in someone. Can suicide, or more likely, can a psychiatric illness which increases the likelihood of suicide be inherited? There is good evidence that the predisposition to psychiatric illness can be inherited and this will increase the risk of suicide. Much of the physiological research on suicides seems to show only that depression is common in them, a fact which psychological studies have also confirmed. Gender plays a major role in determining the choice of suicidal behavior, but this is probably as much a result of social expectations as it is hormonal differences.

However, childhood experiences are probably the most critical factors in determining future suicidal behavior, though the research on these experiences is still in a preliminary stage. The experience of loss, the experience of disorganized and disturbed family life, and the experience of particular types of punishment will probably be found to be very important in increasing the risk of subsequent suicide. The two factors, early loss and the turning of anger inward upon the self resulting in depression, constitute the basic elements of Freud's theory of suicide (Litman, 1966).

CHAPTER 4

The Suicidal Person

Suicide And Mental Illness

Perhaps the most obvious feature of the suicidal person is that he or she is usually psychiatrically disturbed. This does not mean that there are signs of psychiatric disturbance in every suicidal person. But the majority of suicidal people are disturbed, and disturbed people have higher suicide rates.

For example, Barraclough (1972) studied one hundred English suicides and found that sixty four had depressive disorders, twenty one of whom met the strict criteria for recurrent affective disorder. Robins (1981) found that 94 percent of a sample of completed suicides were psychiatrically disturbed, and he later reported, (Robins 1986), that nineteen percent of them were psychotic at the time of their death.

Not all investigators find so many disturbed individuals among samples of suicides. Temoche, et al. (1964) reviewed estimates of the proportion of completed suicides who are disturbed and found a range of 5 to 94 percent. All of the higher estimates involved talking to the relatives and friends of the deceased, and therefore the knowledge that the deceased had just killed himself may have distorted the information provided. Using objective data obtained prior to the death, the estimates of the proportion of disturbed people are much lower, ranging from 5 to 22 percent.

A different approach has been to follow-up patients with specific diagnoses and calculate their suicide rate. Temoche, et al. (1964) found a rate for people who had been psychiatrically hospitalized of 37.0 per 100,000 per year as compared to 9.6 for the general population. Sletten, et al. (1972) calculated suicide rates for ex-psychiatric patients of 830 per 100,000 per year for those who had received a diagnosis of neurotic depression, 190 for psychotic depression, 110 for schizophrenia, 100 for personality disorder, 70 for alcohol and drug abuse, 40 for organic brain syndrome and 20 for mental retardation.

More recently, research has focused on depression, (or affective disorder), in particular. Beck and his associates, (for example, Beck, et al., 1975), have found that depression and, in particular, the cognitive component of depression, *hopelessness*, are strong predictors of suicidal intent. Follow-up studies of patients with bipolar affective disorder, (manic-depressive psychosis), find that about 15 percent of their deaths are from suicide, (as compared to about one percent of deaths for the general population).

The circumstances of the suicidal act differ in nature for those with the various psychiatric disorders. For example, antisocial and alcoholic suicides have been found to have come from broken homes more often, and to have more divorces, more arrests and more social disruptions in general (Robins and O'Neal, 1958). Their suicides were in response to interpersonal stress. In contrast, suicides with affective disorder and organic brain syndrome killed themselves more in response to intrapsychic (personal) problems. In the 1980s, research has been increasingly focused on suicide in those with specific diagnoses.

Research on the biochemical basis for suicide has confirmed the association between psychiatric disorder and suicide (Lester, 1988a). From studies on the brains of completed suicides and the body fluids of attempted suicides, suicidal behavior appears to be associated with abnormal responding of the cortisol secreting system to injections of dexamethasone, lower levels of 5-hydroxyindoleacetic acid, (a breakdown product of serotonin), in the cerebrospinal fluid, and lower levels of serotonin in the central nervous system. These biochemical characteristics resemble those of the typical depressed patient, leading us to conclude that the majority of suicides are suffering from affective disorder.

Virginia Woolf illustrates this association clearly. Virginia suffered from a chronic manic-depressive disorder or, in modern terms, a bipolar affective disorder. Her breakdowns occurred after a severe loss, (such as the death of her mother), and after completing a novel and awaiting its publication. Her suicide note indicated that she was killing herself because she could not bear another severe depression.

CASE 7: Virginia Woolf

Virginia Woolf was a leading literary figure in Great Britain in the early part of this Century. She wrote novels, book reviews for newspapers and magazines and literary criticism. She drowned herself in the River Ouse on March 28th, 1941, at the age of 59. The present chapter is based on a biography written by her nephew, Quentin Bell (1972).

Her Parents and Early Years

The Stephens were originally a family of farmers and merchants from Aberdeenshire in Scotland. Her grandfather was first a lawyer, but then joined the Civil Service in the Colonial Office, working hard for the abolition of slavery. He wrote for the *Edinburgh Review* and other journals. He was shy, pessimistic, convinced of his ugliness, and prone to deny himself any pleasure. If he found something he liked, (like cigars or snuff), he avoided it altogether.

His youngest surviving child was a son, Leslie. Leslie was a nervous delicate boy, his mother's darling, and fond of poetry. He went to Cambridge University and later accepted a fellowship there, becoming an ordained minister in the process which was a pre-requisite for the position. However, he was dissatisfied by the life there and moved to London where he worked as a journalist. He eventually became editor of the *Dictionary of National Biography*.

His first wife was Harriet Thackeray, daughter of the novelist. They had a daughter Laura, who was soon noticed to be psychologically disturbed[1]. Harriet died in childbirth in 1875, on Leslie's forty-third birthday. Leslie soon became close to a friend of his wife, Julia Jackson (Duckworth), recently widowed and with three children. They married on

1. She died in an asylum in 1945.

March 26, 1878. They already had four children by their first spouses, and they had two more, a daughter Vanessa and a son Thoby. They planned no more children, but had two more anyway, Virginia and Adrian.

Virginia was born January 25, 1882, in London, into the upper middle classes, though Bell sees the family as at the lower division of this particular class. (They had seven maidservants but no manservants. They sometimes traveled in a cab but did not keep a carriage.)

Virginia was a pretty child and, though she was slow in leaning to talk, soon showed a precocious brilliance. The children soon decided that Vanessa would be a painter and Virginia a writer. Virginia was later described as eccentric, prone to accidents, witty and easily provoked to furious rages by her brothers and sisters. Virginia, who had become the story teller in the nursery, started a family newspaper in 1891 which she produced weekly for four years.

Childhood was relatively uneventful. They all got whooping cough in 1888, from which they all recovered, though Virginia seemed weaker afterwards. The boys were sent off to school, while the girls were educated at home by their parents and then by a succession of governesses and tutors. They learned drawing, dancing, music, and languages. They vacationed in St Ives, Cornwall.

Since we know that Virginia eventually became psychiatrically disturbed, it is important to look for portents of madness in the family. In 1891, Laura was still living at home. A cousin, J. K. Stephen, received brain damage in an accident in 1886 and subsequently showed signs of madness, in particular, manic euphoria and excitement. Virginia's father had very poor health. He collapsed in 1888, 1890, and 1891. He suffered from insomnia, what he called "fits of the horrors", and worries about his finances.

In 1895, Virginia's mother caught influenza. It was followed by rheumatic fever, and she died on May 5th, 1895. Virginia was thirteen. Her father was sixty-three, a widower for the second time. His grief was great, and he broke down frequently in front of his children. His step-daughter, Stella, stepped in to take over the family and comfort Leslie. The oldest of the step-children, George, now twenty-seven, began to molest Virginia (and continued to do so until she was twenty-two).

Adolescence and the First Breakdown

Virginia's first 'breakdown' occurred in the summer of 1895 soon after her mother's death. Later she remembered the excitability and nervousness, the intolerable depression, a fear of meeting people and hearing voices. She stopped writing her family newspaper.

Stella became engaged in 1896 and was married in April, 1897. She became ill with peritonitis and died in July. Virginia's health deteriorated during this period. There was a fear of going out in the street, but also a fever and rheumatic pains. But there was not a complete breakdown. Soon she was back at lessons, learning Greek and Latin.

Leslie's hearing was deteriorating and a lot of his friends had died. However, he had recovered from his grief, though he remained chronically melancholy. He encouraged the literary interests of his family and turned to Vanessa to run the family. He continued to worry about finances which made life hard for Vanessa who had to fight with him for money to run the household.

Thoby went to Cambridge, and Vanessa and Virginia were introduced to his friends, many of whom later became the nucleus of an intellectual group centered around the Stephens children and known as the Bloomsbury group. Vanessa made more of an effort to 'come out' in society than Virginia, but both thoroughly disliked this and withdrew from the activities as soon as they could.

On their own as Adults

Leslie died after a long illness in February 1904. In May, Virginia had her second breakdown. She heard voices, distrusted Vanessa and her nurses, tried to starve herself and grieved for her father. She tried to kill herself by jumping from a window which was not high enough for her to do much harm. As she recovered, the mental symptoms lessened, leaving her with headaches and neuralgia.

The three children decided to move into a house in Bloomsbury by themselves. They began to have 'At Homes' on Thursday evenings to which many intellectual friends came. Virginia published her first piece in *The Guardian* at the end of 1904, and in 1905 she began her association with *The Times Literary Supplement*. She taught briefly at an evening institute for working men. Then in 1906 on a trip to Greece, Vanessa and Thoby both became ill. Vanessa recovered, but Thoby was misdiagnosed as having malaria and died in November with typhoid fever. Vanessa became engaged to Clive Bell two days later. Interestingly, during these crises, Virginia functioned well and without any breakdown, though she missed Thoby greatly.

After Vanessa's marriage, Virginia and Adrian moved into a smaller house, and their life continued much as before with Thoby's friends as theirs and with activities being split between their household and the Bell's. Virginia's writing was successful, and she began working on a novel in addition to writing for literary magazines. Virginia also began seriously to think of marriage for the first time.

Hitherto, Virginia had been attached mainly to women, especially Violet Dickinson, who seemed to have been in love with Virginia and vice versa, though the relationship was not sexual. Virginia's first flirtation was with an older family friend, Walter Headlam, but the interest soon petered out, and he died unexpectedly in June 1908, causing her some grief.

Virginia was physically ill and close to another breakdown in 1910 but recovered after a rest cure. She turned down a proposal of marriage from Lytton Strachey, (who was homosexual), and resisted the attention of her brother-in-law, Clive. After rejecting several suitors, in 1911, an old friend, Leonard Woolf, returned on leave from Ceylon and fell in love with Virginia. After another bout with exhaustion in 1912, Virginia agreed to marry Leonard. The wedding took place in August, 1912.

Mrs. Woolf

Virginia's life with Leonard was full, but also relatively uneventful. They lived happily together, moved houses, started a publishing company (the Hogarth Press), and worked hard. Virginia wrote, eventually amassing a considerable body of work, including novels that were received with critical acclaim.

Their life quickly developed into a routine. Leonard took care of Virginia, especially during her breakdowns, but also between breakdowns as he tried to prevent their reoccurrence. They wrote most mornings, walked in the afternoons, and read in the evenings. They entertained a lot and were entertained in return.

Virginia was frigid which was ascribed to her experiences with her half-brother. Virginia wanted to have children, though Leonard did not. After much consultation with specialists, the majority opinion was that it was too dangerous for her to have any.

Her first novel (*The Voyage Out*) was accepted in 1913, though it was not published until March 1915. However, its acceptance led to another breakdown. She had anxieties about her writing talent, sleepless nights, headaches, depression, a sense of guilt, an aversion to food, and fears that people were laughing at her. In September, 1913, Virginia took a lethal dose of veronal, but after having her stomach pumped, she survived - barely. As she recovered, her manias returned, and she went from depression to violent excitement. Leonard considered putting her into an asylum, but rejected the idea, and slowly she began to recover, though with a relapse in February, 1915, just before her novel appeared.

The reviews of her novel were positive, and her recovery progressed. Virginia's novels were very close to her own private world, and she was aware that they might be seen as crazy (or really be crazy). If they had been mocked, then this would have been a mockery of her true self. Praise for her novels was a certificate of sanity.

Her Death

Virginia had breakdowns in June 1921, (after a mild depression in August 1919 just before the publication of *Night And Day*), and mild ones in August 1926, September 1929, May 1936. She had frequent periods of total exhaustion, notably January 1922, September 1925, and July 1933, as well as many less severe illnesses.

All of her novels caused her anxiety and depression, especially during the time between the completion of writing and the appearance of the book. Also, beginning in 1934, her style was seen by critics as old-fashioned, and criticism became more common.

As she grew older, more and more friends died. Kitty Maxse killed herself in 1922 and Dora Carrington in 1932. Lytton Strachey died in 1932 and her nephew Julian in 1937 in the Spanish Civil War.

The Second World War also created intense stress for Virginia. (Leonard was Jewish.) They discussed suicide in May 1940, and decided to keep enough gasoline on hand, (and later morphia), to kill themselves.

She finished a final novel (*Between The Acts*) in November 1940. By January, Leonard was alarmed at her psychological state. On the morning of Friday March 28, 1941, Virginia wrote suicide notes and walked to the River Ouse where she put a large stone into her coat pocket and drowned herself, (possibly already having tried to drown herself at an earlier time). In her letter to Leonard, she explained:

> *I feel certain I am going mad again. I feel we can't go through another of those terrible times. And I shan't recover this time. (Bell, 1972, p. 226)*

Analysis

Virginia clearly had recurrent mental breakdowns during her life. It is possible that she indeed suffered from a manic-depressive psychosis, with periods of both depression and mania. She also heard voices and had some phobic behaviors concerned with eating, (even when she was not psychotic). Her breakdowns seemed to have occurred after two types of events: severe loss, (for example, after the death of her mother), and after completing a novel and waiting for its publication.

She was also prone to exhaustion, and her family thought that this was brought on by too much social activity. Typically, a rest cure was prescribed. This exhaustion seemed to facilitate the appearance of a breakdown.

Her suicide note asserted that she was killing herself because she was scared of suffering another breakdown, one with no recovery, and because of the effect of her illnesses on Leonard. Some people go mad to prevent themselves committing suicide; others commit suicide because of their fear of mental illness. Virginia seems to be among the latter.

The question that remains is one of timing. Why in 1941? She almost died in her suicide attempt soon after her marriage when her literary career was still in its infancy. By 1941, however, her novels were receiving increasing criticism, and she feared that she would not be able to write again. The war, with its threats for Leonard, was also a new stress. (Their house in London was damaged by bombs.) She was fifty-nine, perhaps no longer possessing the resiliency of her youth.

She was an agnostic, without religious beliefs that might inhibit her taking her own life. This time, too, there was no attending physician to advise them. Leonard persuaded a friend who was physician to see Virginia. But apart from this one consultation, there was no doctor, therapist or nurse on hand. Four days before her suicide, Virginia wrote to her publishers asking that her novel not be published, indicating that her typical fears about publishing were still strong.

If she had been able to survive this latest breakdown, would she have recovered as she had in the past? And would she eventually have killed herself, perhaps during the next crisis. She was a chronically depressed person, with a history of suicidal preoccupation, and she might have killed herself at any time. As with other cases discussed in this book, it is perhaps a surprise that she lived so long.

◆ ◆ ◆

Suicide and Aggression

The Freudian view of suicide is that it is a response to loss of a loved one, particularly someone with whom you have closely identified. The person is directing the anger, originally felt toward the person who has abandoned you, inward on to the self (Litman, 1966). Edwin Shneidman has called this murder in the 180th degree.

It has been easy, therefore, to conceptualize suicide and murder as opposed behaviors. Depressed and suicidal people are blocking their anger and turning it inward, while assaultive and murderous people are expressing their anger outwards. Henry and Short (1954), for example, felt that people who are subjected to strong external pressures and who can blame these pressures for their misery will aggress outwardly, whereas people free from such pressures and with no one to blame but themselves will be suicidal. In the USA and South Africa, for example, blacks have the higher homicide rates while whites have the higher suicide rates Lester, 1971). Henry and Short also argued that different techniques of punishment lead to the two patterns. The experience of physical punishment in childhood is more likely to produce assaultive people, whereas love-oriented punishment, (Mummy won't love if you do that), is more likely to produce depressed people, (because love-oriented punishment is more likely to produce a child who will inhibit his anger at the punishing parent for fear that to express this anger will *definitely* lead to loss of love).

This has led to the assumption that suicidal people will, on the whole, be non-aggressive people. The research evidence does not support this idea (Lester, 1987e). For example, Conte and Plutchik (1974) found that attempted suicides felt more angry, (and depressed), than non suicidal psychiatric patients. Myers and Neal (1978) found more violent behavior in the histories of completed suicides than of other psychiatric patients, violence both toward others and toward property. Philip (1970) found that attempted suicides had higher hostility scores on a psychological test than normal people or neurotics and did not differ in the direction in which this hostility was expressed.

Furthermore, comparisons of suicides with murderers have identified few personality differences, if any. For example, Lester and Perdue (1974) found that response patterns on the Rorschach ink-blot test identified as characteristic of attempted suicides were equally common in murderers.

Thus, it appears that suicidal people are more aggressive than the average individual and they do not have a general tendency to inhibit anger and turn it inward upon the self.

The Way in Which Suicidal People Think

Those who think suicide is an irrational act have suggested that the thinking process of the suicidal individual must be illogical. Shneidman and Farberow (1957a) suggested that suicidal person confuses the meaning of the word *self.* They confuse the self as experienced by themselves with the self as experienced by others. They act as if they will be around after their death to savor the reactions of others. They forget that will not witness the guilt or affection that others may feel for them after their death.

(Of course, certain religious belief systems lead to the expectation that you will be around somewhere to experience events after your death. Those who commit suicide in order to be reunited with dead loved ones are good illustrations of the danger of some belief systems.)

Neuringer (1988) has focused on more observable thought processes. In a series of studies, he has given suicidal and non-suicidal people a variety of tasks and questionnaires in order to monitor their thinking processes. He has concluded that suicidal people, like most disturbed people, think more dichotomously than normal people. Events are black or white, with no shades of grey possible. Suicidal people also think more rigidly than other disturbed and normal people.

These tendencies can be seen as facilitating the suicidal tendency. In times of distress, whether caused by personal or interpersonal problems, the suicidal person is more likely to catastrophize the situation (Ellis, 1973) and see it as hopeless. The rigidity in thinking will impede the search for alternative solutions to the problem.

Communicating Suicidal Intent

Commonly, when someone kills himself, people who knew the person often express surprise over the suicide. Listening to them, one would assume that the suicidal person made no prior communications about his suicidal behavior. Research shows that this is false.

Robins, et al. (1959) identified twenty-six ways in which suicidal people communicate their intentions, and they found that sixty-nine percent of the sample of completed suicides had communicated their intent. These communications were recent and were given to a wide range of relatives and friends. The communications were sometimes direct, (a chronic alcoholic told his six-year old daughter he was going to kill himself), and sometimes less direct, (a man called his ex-mother-in-law and asked her to light a candle for him). Occasionally, the communication is more subtle. For example, one teenager who completed suicide (Asinof, 1971) cleaned out his room, even removing the posters from the walls, and gave all of his loose change to his sister-in-law. I have often commented in talks on suicide that, if people living with me clean out their rooms and give me their spare money, I would discuss with them the reasons for their actions!

Again, a personal anecdote that I often relate is of a colleague who, on Friday as we left work, responded to my comment "See you Monday," with "Maybe." I wondered about that "Maybe" all the way home, and I called the person when I arrived home and asked if he was depressed and suicidal. Ten years later, he is still alive.

Everyone cannot be sensitive all the time to possible suicidal communications. But the critical question is not why don't suicidal people communicate their intent, (for they do), but rather why don't people hear them.

The answers are various. Sometimes, the significant others are angry toward the suicidal person and, (consciously or unconsciously), want them to die. It is not easy to live with a depressed suicidal person or a chronic alcoholic who is continually threatening suicide. Richman (1986) has documented the many ways in which family members communicate their hostility, and even death wishes, toward the eventual suicide.

Interestingly, both completed suicides and attempted suicides communicate their suicidal intent (and attempted suicide itself can be seen as a method of communication). Beck and Lester (1976) studied the manner of communication and found that, for completed suicides, the issue seemed to be whether to communicate or not. For attempted suicides, on the other hand, the issue seemed to be whether to communicate before or after the suicidal act.

In the life of Judy Garland we can see many signs of prior communication. Judy made innumerable attempts on her life using cutting and overdoses. Those around her knew that the potential for another suicidal action was always very high. She often made these attempts when others were around, which would facilitate intervention.

Judy was also a very demanding and self-centered person so that it would be easy to feel anger toward her. One can imagine saying to such a person if she verbally threatened suicide, "Oh, stop threatening and go ahead," though there is no evidence from her biographer than anyone actually said these words to her. But such wishes might easily have been conscious or unconscious thoughts.

CASE 8: Judy Garland

Judy Garland rose to become a famous movie star and singer. For all of her adult life, she was addicted to drugs, and she made numerous suicide attempts. Judy died from an overdose of sleeping pills in London on June 22, 1969. Her daughter, Liza Minelli, and her biographer (Frank, 1975) both believe that Judy's death was accidental. But this seems very unlikely. We will see that Judy was very likely to kill herself and that in all probability she did.

Childhood

Frank Gumm had been born in Tennessee and his wife Ethel in Michigan. They worked together entertaining movie audiences. After their first two daughters were born, Mary Jane (Suzy) on September 24, 1915, and Virginia (Jimmy) on July 4, 1917, Frank decided to settle down and leased the movie theater in Grand Rapids, Minnesota, supplementing his earnings with a job on the local newspaper. Ethel, helped him, selling tickets and playing the piano during the silent movies. Her daughters sang for the audience during the intermission.

When Ethel got pregnant again, she and Frank decided to have an abortion, but their friend, Marc Rabwin, studying to become a doctor, persuaded them that it was too dangerous. They hoped for a son, but Judy was born two weeks overdue on June 10, 1922, named Frances Gumm. Judy knew that she wasn't wanted, that her parents wanted a son and that she was overdue. Clearly her parents told her of their desires and attitudes, and this must have shaped her negative self-image.

Judy's childhood was reasonably happy. The household was cheerful, and relatives were always around. There was lots of music and singing. And Judy, known as Baby, was the pampered child. When she about a year old, Judy fell ill with a fever and an inability to hold any food down. She recovered after a month in hospital, but nearly died. After this, Judy was seen as delicate and fragile, and this increased the extent to which her family indulged her. Judy was self-willed, she demanded whatever she wanted, and "she was spoiled rotten." A friend of the family who saw Judy when she was five decided she was a tyrant, and wondered how Judy would ever meet disappointment. (Ethel even served Judy's breakfast in bed!)

When she was two-and-a-half, Judy made her stage debut at her father's movie theater, and soon the parents had created an act for the three Gumm sisters. In June 1926, the parents moved to Los Angeles, where their friend Marc Rabwin was now a doctor. Frank leased a movie theater in Lancaster, north of Los Angeles on the edge of the Mojave Desert.

The family lived there for the next six years, from Judy's fifth birthday to her eleventh. Almost as soon as they arrived, Judy fell ill again with a fever. She also suffered from bad hay fever there. Frank and Ethel's marriage deteriorated during this period. Ethel became involved with a married friend, and in fact married him after both of their spouses had died. There is also the possibility that Frank had homosexual tendencies. All that the children knew then was that their parents quarreled a lot and often threatened to separate.

Ethel devoted much attention to her daughters' careers. She enrolled them in the local dance school, she gave them music lessons, and she had them sing. In late 1927, she enrolled them in a dance school in Los Angeles which had been a springboard for many stars. Judy liked this, but she also missed the fun of childhood and disliked the early morning hours and continual lessons. Eventually Suzy and Jimmy dropped out of the weekend lessons in Los Angeles. Ethel took Judy for auditions and was the typical pushy stage-mother. Judy, however, began to enjoy the enthusiastic response of an audience.

The Gumm sisters still performed as an act together, and word began to spread (even in the press) about the child with the incredible voice. They didn't earn a lot from their performances, and this drained the family's earnings. In 1933, the financial problems forced them to give up the movie theater, and they moved to Los Angeles.

Judy was enrolled there in a school for professional children. The Gumm sisters, now called the Garland sisters, continued to perform in the Los Angeles area and elsewhere (including Lake Tahoe). Several people tried to get Judy, as she was now called, a movie contract. She sang for Joe Mankiewicz, she sang for Ida Koverman who worked for Louis B. Mayer (the head of Metro-Goldwyn-Mayer), and soon she sang for Mayer himself, who signed her without a screen test in September, 1935, when she was thirteen.

Early Years at Metro

Metro continued and enlarged upon the pampering and special treatment that Judy had already experienced. Metro's Special Services Department was one of the most extraordinary finishing schools in the world. It provided her education, even building a small classroom near the set when she was working on a movie. She had a voice coach, was given dance lessons, diction lessons, drama lessons, make-up lessons, and deportment lessons, and had a physical therapist and specialists to help her lose weight.

Metro was a factory, designed to turn out fifty-two movies a year to send to their theater chain (Loew's). Three thousand people worked in Culver City making this possible. But, of course, this led to intense scrutiny and competition between the actors. Judy was short, plump, with scoliosis (a slight curvature of the spine which ran in her mother's family). Her teeth were crooked and her nose a problem. (Judy had to wear removable caps on her teeth and rubber discs in her nose on screen.) She also had to continually fight excessive weight above her waist. Judy was humiliated by all of these judgments and by comparison with her peers. Judy soon came to believe that she was not physically attractive or sexually desirable to men, and certainly inferior to the other teenagers there (who included Lana Turner, Elizabeth Taylor and Hedy Lamarr). Ethel would remind Judy that she was signed for her voice, but that was not enough for Judy.

Judy's voice coach, Roger Edens, worked with her intensively and developed her skills as a singer. And Ethel came to the studio every day to rehearse and accompany her. But seven weeks after Judy signed with Metro, her father died without warning (of a massive hemorrhage of the mastoid). Judy took the pillow her father had lain on and slept on it for many nights, resisting all efforts to wash it. His death was a profound shock for her, and she spent much of her life looking for a father figure to replace him. Most of her close friends were males, and she was truly happy only when she was in love.

Her first two roles were in a short movie *Every Sunday* with Metro and a small part in *Pigskin Parade* for Twentieth Century Fox. Her first major movie role was in *Broadway Melody of 1938*, and for this movie the studio began giving Judy benzedrine and phenobarbital to help her lose weight and to sleep at nights. These were new wonder drugs for the movie colony in California, and no one was aware of their addictive potential. For Judy, their use for *Broadway Melody* began her life-long dependence on drugs.

Broadway Melody was released in the Fall of 1937, and the reviews of Judy's performance were enthusiastic. After several more movies, usually with Judy cast as the girl who never gets the man she loves, MGM decided to build a movie especially for Judy, *The Wizard of Oz.*

Work on *The Wizard of Oz* began in mid 1939. Judy first showed her need for privacy on the set of this movie. She stayed in her dressing room a lot, even taking her three hours of school lessons there rather than in the teaching cubicle usually built on the set. The movie was released in August, and Judy went on a publicity tour with Mickey Rooney. Before one performance, Judy collapsed backstage and couldn't go on, the first of many such collapses in her life as a performer.

In November, Ethel eloped with Will Gilmore, her long-time lover now recently widowed, to Arizona where she married him on the fourth anniversary of Frank Gumm's death. Judy never forgave her mother for this.

Although Judy had several crushes, her first love was Artie Shaw, in his late twenties and twice divorced. She confided to him her self-doubts. She saw herself as homely, fat and ugly. She was well aware of the vibrato in her voice that could get out of control. Artie was never aware that Judy was in love with him. He never thought of Judy as someone to love or make love to. In February 1940, Judy read in the newspapers that Artie had eloped with Lana Turner (who was one of Judy's rivals at Metro). Judy loved him and had seen him three nights before his elopement and had no idea that he was in love with anyone else. Although they remained friends, she felt that he had foresaken her, just as her father had done almost five years earlier.

Judy's adolescence was drawing to a close. In the Spring of 1940 she received a special Oscar for the best juvenile performance (in *The Wizard of Oz*). Later that year, Louis Mayer gave her an eighteenth birthday party at his house, and raised her salary from $750 to $3000 a week. She fell in love with David Rose, the leader of his own orchestra, and married him in July 1941, after fights with her mother about her affair with him. It was Judy who pushed for the marriage. She loved him, but she also wanted to get away from her mother's control. And thus begins the end.

It seems strange to see Judy's life beginning its decline at age nineteen. Although she was a major star already, many of her famous performances were still ahead of her. But her life from now on was simply a repetition. The same events, catastrophes, and breakdowns simply keep reoccurring again and again, except with increasing seriousness. Let us look at the major themes.

Her Mother

Ethel had shaped Judy's life and continued to try to maintain control. She was opposed to most of Judy's loves and lovers.

Ethel's marriage to Will increased the alienation Judy felt, though that marriage lasted less than four years. After a serious row in 1949, Ethel moved to Dallas to live near to her daughter Jimmy. She moved back to Los Angeles eventually to try to help Judy, but Judy refused to see her. She left word with servants not to admit Ethel even to see Liza or Lorna. Ethel died in January 1953, in Los Angeles after a heart attack in the parking lot of the factory where she worked for $61 a week. Judy, of course, went to the funeral and added grief and guilt to the anger she had long felt toward Ethel.

Later in 1962, Judy had a bad argument with her sister Jimmy, and they were never reconciled.

Marriages

Her marriage with David Rose was soon over. Their careers kept them busy and apart. They had different life styles, and Judy's dependence on the drugs was a problem. They separated in the Spring of 1943 and divorced in 1944.

She next married Vincente Minelli in 1945. Vincente made her feel that she was an attractive woman, and he admired her talent as an actress. Liza was born in March 1946, and Judy had problems coping with a husband, a house, a child and a career, especially while addicted to drugs. The marriage deteriorated, and Judy moved out in December 1950. The divorce was final in March 1952.

She married Sidney Luft in June 1952, already pregnant with Lorna who was born in November 1952. (Joey was born in 1955, at which time Judy had her tubes tied.) Sid devoted himself to Judy. He abandoned his career in order to manage Judy's. But marital conflicts grew over the years and in 1958 they separated and began a seven year period of fights, reconciliations and separations. Finally, they were divorced in 1965, whereupon Judy married Mark Herron, a younger man. This marriage lasted only six months before they separated. There was then a succession of possible husbands and affairs until she married another younger man, Mickey Deans, in January 1969. Five months later Judy was dead.

Judy's Career

By the time she was twenty-two, Judy had been in nineteen films. For 1943 through 1945 she was voted one of the five most popular screen actresses. However, Judy's drug and emotional problems began to interfere with her work. She was usually late to work, if she arrived, and temperamental to work with. MGM paid a psychiatrist to be with her on the set in 1947. MGM had to suspend her frequently and fired her from three movies (including *Annie Get Your Gun*). In September 1950, MGM cancelled her contract, almost fifteen years to the day after they signed her.

Judy had always had little or no ability to handle her financial affairs. Her mother and financial advisers had tried to plan wisely but failed. After her divorce from Minelli and her firing from MGM, Judy was continually in debt. In 1950, she and Minelli owed $60,000 in back taxes and thousands more to friends. (In 1966, Judy's assets were listed as $12,000 and her liabilities to 120 creditors were $122,000.)

In 1950, Judy was free from contractual obligations. She could do radio, concerts and films at will. During most of this period she was married to Sidney Luft, and he often acted as a business manager for her. Her freedom was, however, superficial. She was in debt so often that she had to work in order to pay her bills. However, her drug addiction and increasing psychological disturbance led her to cancel performances and walk out on contracts, so that often she could not even cover the expenses of the tour she had embarked on.

She appeared in *A Star Is Born* in 1954, *Judgment At Nuremberg* in 1961, *A Child Is Waiting* in 1962, followed by *I Could Go On Singing*. And she continued to give concerts, some outstanding and others where she was booed off the stage, (as in Australia in 1964), collapsed on stage, or simply went to sleep in the middle of a song.

Drugs and Breakdowns

Judy was addicted to uppers and downers, amphetamines and barbiturates. Severe addiction to amphetamines leads to paranoid symptoms, and Judy developed increasingly severe paranoia. (In her separations from Sid Luft, she was often convinced that he was going to kidnap her children.) In addition, she was an alcoholic. (Judy and Sid attended one meeting of Alcoholics Anonymous and one of Drugs Anonymous but did not like them.) She also smoked heavily, often while drugged, with the result that she set fire to her house on one occasion and to her hotel room on another.

She had frequent stays in hospital and sanitariums, mainly to "dry out" after a physical or psychological collapse: July 1947, March 1949 where she received six electroconvulsive shock treatments, May 1949, November 1951, and more. Eventually, her alcohol and drug abuse caused her liver to become diseased, and she was frequently hospitalized with kidney and liver problems, (for example, in 1959, April 1962, and August 1963), though it is hard to be sure whether she was hospitalized for physical illnesses, to dry out from drugs, or as a result of a suicide attempt.

Judy's Mental And Physical State

Judy suffered from many symptoms, including insomnia, chronic colitis, post-partum depressions, (exacerbated by having to dry out during the pregnancy), headaches, and sudden inexplicable fears (a sense of impending doom, an inability to work, and a fear that she might lose her voice). She frequently collapsed on stage (for example, at The Palace in New York in November 1951).

In 1943, she entered psychoanalysis with Ernst Simmel, but, on her own admission, chronically lied to him and so probably got little benefit from it. He died in the Fall of 1947, another loss for her.

Suicide

It had always been known that her father's Aunt Mary had killed herself by pushing her wheelchair off a bridge because she was dying from a mysterious crippling disease and didn't want to be a burden to her fiancé. Judy's mother made at least one suicide attempt after a fight with Judy, taking a lethal dose of seconal and whiskey, and her stomach had to be pumped.

Judy's sister Suzy attempted suicide with an overdose in the Fall of 1962, (an alcoholic, she had been depressed), and finally killed herself with an overdose in May 1964 while Judy lay recovering from an attempt at suicide with an overdose herself in Hong Kong.

Judy made numerous suicide attempts; in July 1947 after a row with Minelli when she cut her wrists while others were in the house; in June 1950 after another row with Minelli and after being fired from a movie, when she tried to cut her throat; after the birth of Lorna in December 1952 when she cut her throat with a razor; in the 1950s she called a friend threatening to kill herself and her son Joey; in 1957 when she slashed her wrists deeply in the presence of her husband Sid; when she tried to jump out of a window in front of a friend in May 1961; when she took an overdose (or had a kidney attack) in July 1961; when she took an overdose in London in July 1962 (and later paid a blackmailer to keep the photographs out of the press); in September 1962 when she took another overdose (or had another kidney attack); when she took a large overdose in Hong Kong in May 1964 during a typhoon in Hong Kong and had her stomach pumped; when she threatened to jump out of the window in front of Mark Herron in 1965; when she slashed her face superficially in 1966 after a row with Mark (and claimed he had cut her); when she overdosed in March 1969 while on a concert tour in Scandinavia; and finally when she killed herself with an overdose in June 1969.

(Judy often seemed to have no memory of her attempts, and her biographer wanted to believe that Judy attempted suicide only under the influence of drugs. She also usually went to the bathroom for her slashings and overdoses.)

At the time of her death she had just married Mickey Deans, a young pianist-singer who had been managing a discotheque in Manhattan. They married in London in January, 1969, and again in March in case there had been a delay in her divorce from Mark Herron. Judy was still giving concerts and went to Scandinavia in the Spring for a series. Judy and Mickey flew to New York in May, where her daughter Liza found her subdued and very thin. A physician called in by a friend tried to take her off seconal and switch her to thorazine. Judy and Mickey flew back to London on June 17th after Mickey's plan to open a chain of Judy Garland Theaters in America had fallen through.

At 2 am in California on the 22nd of June, a friend (John Carlyle) called her in London (where it was 10am) to talk to her. Mickey looked for her and found her in the bathroom, dead from an overdose.

Analysis

There is much in Judy's life of interest given her eventual suicide - a history of chronic alcohol and drug abuse, severe depressions and suicidal behavior, and problems in her marriages and relationships with friends made worse by her drug addiction. Several of these deserve discussion.

Loss

Judy experienced many losses in her life. Her father died when she was thirteen, her first love never even realized that she was in love with him and married a rival teenage star. Her mother died. Her sister killed herself. Even her psychoanalyst died.

In addition, her severe illnesses when she was a year old and when she was five meant separations from her mother which may have made these later losses more difficult to adjust to.

Suicide

Her daughter Liza did not want to believe that Judy's death was suicidal, and neither did her biographer. It is clear that Judy had a chronic history of suicidal behavior, much of it nonlethal and almost always done while others were around. However, several attempts were lethal, requiring stomach pumping and intensive care. She could easily have died during those attempts. And one of her wrist slashings when Sid was present was very deep.

Thus, although it is clear that her suicidal behavior could be seen as impulsive, manipulative and a cry for help, this does not eliminate the possibility that Judy also, at times, truly wanted to die.

Furthermore, the timing of her final suicidal act is important. Her career and life had been disintegrating at a fast rate. She was going through lovers and husbands quite quickly, arguing with them soon after going to bed with them. She was no longer seeking father figures, but taking any new young man who was around and would bolster her self-esteem. She had been drunk and fallen asleep on stage and been booed. She was heavily in debt.

How many more friends could she find who would put up with her incredible demands? What had she to look forward to? Who would marry her next? Even her children were disengaging themselves from her.

Her existence was ready for death.

The Real Judy and the Pampered Star

Judy Garland was spoiled and immature. She behaved like a small child. She was incapable of caring for others or of taking care of them. These traits became more extreme as she got older, but were always there. Let me give some illustrations.

In 1963, Judy wanted her daughter Liza to be with her in California. But Liza was in her fourth month of *Best Foot Forward* in New York and in love with a dancer. Judy called and offered the dancer a part on her television show. When he flew to California, Liza quit her show and went to California too. When Judy wanted something, she demanded it, now and at any cost to others.

(Of course, she was also jealous of Liza's growing success, as well as proud, and the chance of interfering with Liza's career probably played a part too, especially as her own career was in ruin.)

Judy called friends at all hours of the night to talk because she could not sleep or to summon them to her house. When she needed someone to talk at 3 am, she didn't care that they had to go to work at 6 am. She fired her doctors when they balked at 2 am calls. Judy would even keep her children awake to keep her company. Lorna and Joey would be tired, but Judy would keep them awake and talk, talk, talk through the night.

In fact, Liza and Lorna had always served as therapists for Judy. They grew up to be what psychologist call "parentalized children", children who never got to experience a healthy childhood in which they can depend upon others to take care of them, but rather childhoods in which they have to take care of parents. No wonder that Judy's children needed psychotherapy!

The luckiest choice she made in her lovers was Sid Luft. He devoted his life to her completely for a while. Her needs for love, attention and affection could never be satisfied, but Sid thought that he alone could do it. Even after the bitter break-up of the marriage, Judy could still turn to him, and he could not resist her entreaties.

Again, Judy's irresponsibility in all matters got worse toward the end of her life. But an example from this period epitomizes her. When in New York in 1967, Lorna, then fourteen, was running the house, looking after her mother, picking out clothes for her and so on. One night, Judy decided to cook a meal. First she needed money. She sent friends out to borrow $200 from her ex-husband Sid. Amazingly, he gave them the money! The shopping list began with an electric meat grinder, twelve crystal goblets and twelve liqueur glasses at one of the most expensive stores in Manhattan. And then they bought the food. But Judy decided not to bother grinding the meat. She told them to call Sid and have him buy some ground meat. He did! Judy opened a can of gravy (the extent of her cooking), and they sat down to eat at 11 pm.

Of course, Judy in the 1960s was a caricature of what she had been, but she had not been too different when younger. As the young star, even before she signed with MGM, Judy saw the world as revolving around her.

But who was she? To a large extent, she was a creation first of her mother and then of the studio. She had been shaped and directed by others. Her reward was attention, praise, and eventually applause. Ethel disapproved of much of what Judy herself wanted. Thus, Ethel would not let Judy explore her own desires but always tried to impose her own will. This was especially evident over Judy's boy friends and lovers, and eventually Judy had no choice but to break with her.

But by this time, Judy's real self had been neglected to such an extent that all she could seek in her independence was continual support for the social self she had developed. Thus, she needed admiring friends, lovers and husbands, and drugs to keep her from ever exploring herself, the Judy that saw herself as fat and ugly with a precarious voice.

Judy Garland, the star, was worth something. Frances Gumm was a frightening, dreadful and appalling prospect. Judy Garland could command others to obey her whims. Frances Gumm couldn't even choose clothes to wear, form healthy relationships, or earn a decent living out there in the real world.

Like Ernest Hemingway and Marilyn Monroe, (and to a lesser extent others, such as Hart Crane), Judy Garland lied about and distorted her past. She tried especially to put the blame on others for her misfortunes and failures. The callous studio. The nasty mother. All to bolster the public Judy and avoid dealing with the real Frances.[5]

We can see that, at the age of forty-seven, it was proving increasingly difficult for Judy to continue her life-style. She could no longer support the image that had been created.

Her choice was between finally discovering and exploring Frances Gumm and replacing Judy Garland with this real self, or dying. She chose to die.

◆ ◆ ◆

Judy's biographer and her relatives (including her daughter Liza) denied that Judy's death was suicide. (It is interesting that people often rumor that someone's death is suicide, unless it appears that it was suicide in which case people deny that it was suicide. Marilyn Monroe was murdered, Sylvia Plath's death was a suicide attempt that went wrong, Jack London's death was an accidental overdose, and so on.)

Why is this? Denial of the deceased person's suicidal intent serves to lessen your guilt over their death. If their death was suicide, it seems to reflect on you. Why didn't you intervene to save them? What did you do that drove them to death? Increasingly, research is focussing on the effects (including the stigma) on the survivors of someone else's suicide (Rudestam, 1989).

---

5. For example, a time when she and her sisters had collected bees became a story of how her sisters had locked her in a room with bees which stung her.

The Suicide Note

Suicidal people leave very little information behind. Occasionally there is a case record in a hospital, sometimes a diary. But about thirty five percent of suicides do leave suicide notes. Some leave short notes, others long notes; some leave one, others many.

Jacobs (1967) noted that the most common form of suicide note was one in which the person indicates that he is suffering from extremely distressing problems of long duration, that death is the only solution, and that those left behind should forgive him even though they may not understand his decision. Typically he asks for forgiveness. If the person is suffering from a severe illness, these features may be stressed less since he knows the survivors will understand his suicidal choice more easily.

Less common are notes that express the anger of the suicidal person toward others. In addition, many notes are concerned with instructions to the survivors and bequests.

In 1957, Shneidman and Farberow (1957b) published 33 genuine suicide notes matched with 33 simulated notes written by individuals who were not contemplating suicide. These notes have generated a great deal of research. For example, Spiegel and Neuringer (1963) found that genuine notes were less likely to include the word "suicide" and were less explicit about intentions, had more instructions, and were more disorganized.

However, it far from clear what these studies have told us. Rather than finding out about suicidal people, perhaps all we have learned is how nonsuicidal people conceive of the suicidal state (Lester, 1988e)?

More recently, Leenaars (1988) has taken ten theorists of personality, (including Sigmund Freud, Alfred Adler and Carl Jung), and theorists of suicide, (such as Karl Menninger and Edwin Shneidman), operationalized their theory of suicide and searched for evidence of the themes in suicide notes. Some theorists proved to be quite successful in characterizing the content of genuine suicidal notes, (Karl Menninger, Henry Murray, Edwin Shneidman, Harry Sullivan, and Gregory Zilboorg), while others were of no use (Ludwig Binswanger and George Kelly).

The Personality of Suicidal People

There have been a great number of studies of the personality of suicidal people, but few reliable differences have emerged. One clear and obvious finding is that suicidal people are more psychologically disturbed than non suicidal people (Lester, 1988a). There is good evidence that suicidal people are more depressed and, in particular, hopeless, as we have discussed above in this chapter. Suicidal people have lower self-esteem and a more positive attitude toward death. However, on personality traits such as a belief in an external locus of control, (whether you believe that what happens to you is result of external forces or your own performance), intelligence and risk-taking there are no consistent results yet (Lester, 1972, 1983).

Suicidal Types

One approach to this lack of consistency in research on the personality of suicidal people has been to search for suicidal types. There are many bases for a typology of suicidal people, including psychiatric disorder. Several investigators have devised empirical types based upon statistical analyses of data obtained from large samples of suicidal people. Bagley, et al. (1976) identified three types: chronically depressed, sociopathic, and the old and handicapped.

However, the more interesting typologies have looked at life-styles. These are often "arm-chair" typologies, devised by authors based upon their clinical experience. For example, Baechler (1979) described the escapist, (one who flees from an intolerable situation), the aggressive, (who seeks vengeance by inducing remorse in the survivors), the oblative, (who sacrifices himself to attain some goal), and the ludic, (who seeks an ordeal through risk taking).

At the present time, none of the clinically derived typologies have been validated by empirical research and none of the empirical typologies have been validated by independent researchers. Much research needs to be done here.

CHAPTER 5

The Social Context Of Suicide

Suicide takes place in a social context. The suicidal individual has a network of relatives and friends and lives in society with particular norms and values. This chapter will examine how these social factors influence the rate and the type of suicidal acts that take place.

Durkheim on Suicide

The first influential sociologist to write about suicide was Emile Durkheim in France in 1897 (Durkheim, 1951). His influence has been so great in sociological research into suicide that his volume on suicide is treated almost like a Bible, and sociologists seem more willing to investigate hypothesis suggested by Durkheim than those suggested by more modern theorists.

Durkheim proposed that two basic concepts could explain much of suicidal behavior. First, people differ in the degree to which they are integrated into society. People have differing numbers of relatives and friends and different strengths of relationship with these people. They also differ in the extent to which they belong to community, national and professional groups.

Durkheim described two types of suicides who are too well socially integrated or not sufficiently integrated. Those who were too well integrated committed *altruistic suicide*, in which they sacrificed their lives for others. Those who were not sufficiently socially integrated committed *egoistic suicide*.

The second concept Durkheim focused on was that of social regulation, the degree to which our thoughts, desires, emotions and behaviors are regulated by society. *Anomic suicide* is committed by those who are under-regulated by society, while *fatalistic suicide* is committed by those who are over-regulated by society.

There is also the assumption that the rate of suicide will vary with the degree of social integration and social regulation, and to be consistent, we would have to argue that the relationship is curvilinear, with the highest rates occurring at very high or very low levels of both social integration and social regulation.

Or perhaps we should classify societies on both dimensions simultaneously, producing the following classification:

parents. Their homes fostered low self-esteem and feelings of chronic insecurity and taught them by example that interpersonal relationships were unreliable and punishing.

The women described their adolescent years as unhappy. Their homes were filled with conflict and tension. They felt isolated from family and friends and different from their peers. They performed poorly in school, which fed into their low self-esteem. One group, primarily lower class, overconformed and became dependent and passive, feeling at fault for the conflicts around them. They tried to be good girls. Another group, mainly middle class, became defiant and rebellious and misbehaved. They tried to be bad.

In adulthood three styles emerged in their interactions with lovers and husbands. One style consisted of intense dependency upon the partner, an inability to face disappointment without hurt, and the need for constant proof of his love and affection. Her sexual intimacy usually preceded the suicide attempt.

Some of the women were involved with men, often substance abusers, who physically abused them. The women usually blamed themselves for the attacks and attempted suicide [illegible] and to take revenge.

[illegible]

CHAPTER 6

Suicide In Special Groups

From time to time, the media (and scholars too) become interested in suicide in special groups. The focus has been on the American Indians, blacks, the elderly, teenagers, drug abusers, alcoholics, celebrities, and so on. Most of these interest are short lived, and few generate much meaningful research. Three groups, however, have aroused sustained concern.

Some groups of American Indians have had high suicide rates for many years, and concern for this problem has been steady, not subject to temporary shifts in media attention. It is a problem on which psychiatrists and anthropologists can join together in investigating, and there is now a journal devoted to mental health problems among American Indians (*The White Cloud Journal*).

Suicide in adolescents has been of concern in recent years because their suicide rate has been increasing in the United States. Suicide in adolescents seems to be such a waste of life, and it is a great puzzle to us. Adolescents who commit suicide seem to have insufficient reasons to do so from our adult perspective.

Drug abuse is also of great concern today, less because we are concerned about drug abusers, I think, but more because we fear drug abuse affecting more and more of the members of our society, especially our children and relatives. Eliminating drug abuse is a priority of almost every politician responding to public demand, (though legalizing drug use remains a minor theme). Drug abuse is a self-destructive behavior in itself, and drug abusers do have a high rate of suicide.

In this chapter I will examine suicide in each of these three groups in some detail and illustrate the research with case studies for two of the groups.

Native Americans

In the 1970s, a great deal of media publicity was given to suicide among native Americans (American Indians and native Americans living in the Arctic regions). Occasional reports of suicide rates ten to twelve times the suicide rates for white Americans appeared (for example, Shore, et al., 1972).

Closer examination of the data revealed that while some reservations had very high suicide rates, (for example the Apaches), others had very low rates (for example, the Pima). Overall, the suicide rate was not very different from that of white Americans. Ogden, et al. (1970) found that the crude suicide rate of American Indians overall was about 1.0 to 1.6 times that of the general population, while the age-adjusted suicide rate was about 1.3 to 2.1 times that of the general population.

The crude suicide rates for 1980 show few overall differences between whites and American Indians:

	total suicide rate	male suicide rate	female suicide rate
whites	13.2	20.6	6.1
American Indians	13.0	21.2	4.9

Later investigators have, therefore, studied particular groups of American Indians and looked for differences between the different groups. For example, van Winkle and May (1986) investigated suicide among the Apache, the Navajo and the Pueblo Indians in New Mexico. The crude suicide rates for these three Indian groups for 1957 to 1979 were:

Apache	43.3
Pueblo	27.8
Navajo	12.0

The suicide rates of the three groups fluctuated from 1957 to 1979, but the population size of the three groups is so small that yearly rates are quite unreliable. Although the relative standings of the three groups has remained stable, the rates appear to have risen in all three groups since the late 1960s.

Suicide among these three groups is predominantly a male behavior, with 89.8 percent of the suicides men. The male to female suicide rate ratio is 8.8 to 1. The most common age is 20-24 and the median age of all the suicides is 25.9. The median age of Apache suicides (21.5) was the lowest, with the Pueblo having a median age of 25.1 and the Navajo 27.4.

Three quarters of the Apache suicides were unmarried, as compared to just over half of the Pueblo suicides and only a third of the Navajo suicides.

In seeking to account for suicide rates among American Indians, van Winkle and May used the concepts of social integration (from Durkheim) and acculturation. The Apache were originally nomadic hunters and gatherers, organized into self-sufficient bands whose leaders held limited power. Today, the strongest social tie, the raiding group, has been eliminated, and they live in homes scattered about the reservation or in border towns, raising livestock or working for wages in tribally owned businesses. Religion was never very important for the Apache and continues to play a minor role. Thus, the Apache have had their social integration weakened in modern times.

Although the Navajo were also nomadic hunters and gatherers, they later settled down in hogans (houses with earthen walls supported by timbers) throughout their territory. The matrilineal clans had a strong influence and religion was more important in their lives than for the Apache. Their life now continues to be more socially integrated than that of the Apache because of the continuing influence of local groups and religion. Thus, their lower suicide rate seems to result from this increased social integration.

The Pueblo engaged in agriculture, were very strongly religious, and discouraged individualism. They appear to have been the most strongly integrated of the three groups, and this continues to be the case. Why then is their suicide rate higher than that of the Navajo? Examination of the individual Pueblo groups shows that the groups which have become more acculturated have the higher suicide rates.

Acculturation is occurring in all three groups. The influence of the mass media permeates all groups, and roads have been built to and within all of the reservations. In particular, the reservations of the Apaches are small and surrounded by white communities, and many Apache live in mixed communities. This increasing acculturation may be responsible for the rising suicide rates in all three groups during the 1970s since their exposure to the values of the mainstream culture has shaken their adherence to their traditional values without yet creating a new healthy set of values for them to live by.

Adolescents

Bakwin (1957) reviewed the research on suicide in children and adolescents and found only five recent articles of importance. In the thirty years since then we have witnessed a tremendous increase in concern about suicide in adolescents and an accompanying surge in scholarly articles on the problem.

Two facts have motivated this change. First, it was recognized that suicide is a leading cause of death in young people, exceeded only by accidents and murder (Rosenberg, et al., 1987). Suicide, therefore, is an appropriate target for reducing the death rate in adolescents and an excellent index of their psychological health. The US Public Health Service (1980) has chosen the reduction of the adolescent suicide rate as one of its objectives for the 1980s.

Secondly, the adolescent suicide rate has been rising in recent years. Maris (1985) has provided the following adolescent suicide rates:

	1970	1980
white males	13.9	21.4
white females	04.2	04.6
black males	10.5	12.3
black females	03.8	02.3

It is interesting to note that just as suicide rates are highest in elderly white males, adolescent suicide rates have been rising most in young white males. Lester (1988f) has shown that this increasing suicide rate in adolescents is not found in all nations of the world. In some nations, (such as Hong Kong and Portugal), the suicide rate of youth hardly rose at all from 1970 to 1980, in some, (such as Norway and Spain), the rate rose dramatically, while in others, (such as Guatemala and Venezuela), the rate dropped.

When one reads the recent burgeoning literature on suicide in adolescents, it is disheartening to find that much of it adds little to our understanding of why adolescent suicide rates are increasing. However, there are some interesting leads being developed.

First, when psychologists write about adolescent suicide, they often focus on death wishes in the parents. In general, adolescents who act defiantly are often viewed as acting-out the desires, (conscious or unconscious), of their parents. Richman (1986) has documented vividly the evident desires of parents that their child kill himself. As one father put it to his daughter "at least we'd know where you are" (Rosenbaum and Richman, 1970). In the recent film, *Stand By Me*, a father whose first born son has died in an accident makes his younger son feel that it ought to have been him that died instead!

More generally, investigators of adolescent suicide focus on the family conflicts. Jacobs (1971) has documented how the homes of suicidal adolescents are often

More generally, investigators of adolescent suicide focus on the family conflicts. Jacobs (1971) has documented how the homes of suicidal adolescents are often characterized by excessive instability. For example, not only are divorces in their parents common, but their parents tend to go through more than one marriage. Their parents also tended to use maladaptive control techniques, (such as nagging and yelling), more, and the adolescents showed more behavioral problems, especially withdrawal, (such as running away from home). Closer in time to the suicidal act, the adolescent's remaining social relationships typically dissolve, (such as a romance breaking up), leading the adolescent to feel that he has reached the end of hope.

It is commonly agreed that the adolescent suicide is depressed, as is the adult suicide. But it is also agreed upon that the depression is harder to diagnose since the symptoms are different in adolescents (Greene and Keown, 1986). Depressed adolescents may be irritable, unreasonably angry, or antisocial, behaviors that are common in normal adolescents during the crisis of adolescence. Depressed adolescent boys may choose violence and vandalism, while the girls may become promiscuous. Substance abuse may also signal depression. These symptoms may be accompanied by poor school performance and physical complaints of recurrent chest, stomach or head pain.

As mentioned in the previous chapter, Phillips (1974) has shown that the publicized suicides of others often leads to a temporary increase in the suicide rate. Adolescents are especially sensitive to these influences, and "epidemics" or clusters of adolescent suicides have occurred in schools. For example, Lester (1987h) presented the case of three adolescents out of a group of five who committed suicide in one school in Pennsylvania and whose deaths precipitated suicidal behavior and psychological distress in several other adolescents in the school.

Psychiatric illness is often found in adolescents. Judgments of the incidence of psychiatric illness in suicides are very sensitive to the biases and prejudices of the diagnostician, and no good study has appeared comparing the incidence of psychiatric illness in adolescents and adults by the same diagnostician so that at least the bias will be similar for both groups.

However, what is puzzling is that severe psychiatric illness is often absent. The result is that the adolescent's suicide does not make sense to us. It seems under-determined, that is, there are simply not sufficient reasons to account for it. This problem is made worse by the fact that adolescent suicide often does not follow the same patterns as adult suicide. For example, the temporal variation, (over days of the week and month of the year), is often not found (Frank and Lester, 1988a). Or again, whereas national adult suicide rates are related to the quality of life in those nations, adolescent suicide rates are not (Lester, 1988f).

There are many adolescent suicides who have had their biographies written (often by their mothers). I have chosen one who does not appear to have been severely psychiatrically disturbed so that we must puzzle out the causes of his suicide without recourse to simply dismissing him as crazy.

CASE 11: Jody White

Jody White shot himself at the age of seventeen, and his story is told by his mother (White-Bowden, 1985). His mother Susan had married secretly when she was fifteen to John White, eight years her senior. They had two children, both girls, and then Susan became pregnant again. John did not want a third child and pushed Susan to have an illegal abortion. (Legal abortions were not possible then.) She refused and had the child, Jody, on March 8, 1960. Majorie was then four and O'Donnell seventeen months.

The family lived in a house that they had built on Susan's family farm. The marriage soon deteriorated. Indeed, Susan realized on the honeymoon that she had made a mistake in marrying John, but she did not ask her parents to get the marriage annulled. (She hoped they would suggest it to her.) Susan and John disagreed about everything, and John dominated the decisions. John had several affairs, and there were several separations before a final divorce. Susan describes her sex life as good but felt a lack of open and honest communication between her and John. John had a management job for a construction company and worked weekends on his own airplane.

Early Years

His mother describes Jody as a placid, easy and happy child. Jody had a speech impediment in which he left off the initial consonants of words. His father tried to correct him quite harshly, preventing him from eating, for example, until he correctly pronounced the words. After Jody was ridiculed at school, his mother took him to a speech therapist who helped Jody correct the problem.

Susan and her daughters spoiled Jody, except on the rare occasions when John was home. John wanted his son to be strong, unemotional and mature. He forbade everyone in the family to hug and kiss Jody and punished Jody for giggling and crying.

However, when Jody was eight, he and his father began to get close. Jody wanted a mini-bike, and his father told him to save his allowance for one and then helped him buy one. They rode together and fixed the bikes together. Soon Jody was competing in bike races and winning his class. His father was still punitive though, screaming at Jody when he lost.

After the Divorce

Jody's parents got divorced when he was fourteen, after four years of separations and reconciliations. His mother had already begun working, and at the time of the divorce had established herself as a reporter for a local television station. This meant quite long hours, and she could not leave work until after the early evening news. She had also fallen in love with a fellow reporter there (Jack Bowden).

Jody's father refused to accept the finality of the divorce. He often came over to the family's house and tried to push for another reconciliation. One day in November, 1974, John White was home when Susan arrived. John tried once more to persuade Susan to let him return, telling her that he could not live without her. After dinner, while Susan was taking a bath, John shot himself in her bedroom with a handgun.

In retrospect, Susan feels that she didn't share her feelings with her children and get them to talk about their feelings after this trauma. (Jody did not cry at the funeral.) She didn't think of getting counseling for the family. (O'Donnell and Majorie went for counseling later in their lives.) But they coped and tried to get on with life. Jody and O'Donnell went back to school, and Majorie took a year off before going to college. Jody continued to race his bikes, and his mother took up bike riding and accompanied him to the races on weekends. Jody did not seem depressed at all.

Jody was successful at his bike riding, had a good group of friends and some female admirers. He was shy though, and disliked talking on the telephone. His shyness seemed to worsen as he entered adolescence.

About three months after the father's suicide, Susan had to go to a party at the television station and, since O'Donnell was also going out, Jody had to stay home by himself. He got upset, hung up the telephone when his mother called him from the party, and Susan rushed home to see what was wrong. She expected him to have killed himself, and she was relieved to find him alive. But she felt guilt over abandoning him and promised him not to do it again. (She also felt guilty that she bought Jody whatever he needed, especially bikes and cars, whereas his father would have made him work for them and earn them to some extent.)

When he turned fifteen, Jody moved up to the next class in bike racing and didn't win so often. Jody seemed quite happy that year. He and his mother seemed close, and they would often ride bikes together just for fun. Majorie went off to college in New England, and the family seemed to be coping well. Jack Bowden visited frequently with his son, Christopher, aged six.

Jody had a girl friend that year, a thirteen year old who also rode bikes, but by the time he was sixteen Jody had fallen in love with Lauren, a girl who at first chased Jody, but then rebelled against his possessiveness and caused him much anguish. When she would refuse to go out with him, Jody would sometimes wait outside her house to see if she went out with someone else, in the same way his father had when dating Susan White.

At the end of the school year, Jody messed up some library book cards and unscrewed some fixtures at the private school he attended. Since he at first denied doing so, the school expelled him for breaking their honor code. However, Jody told his mother that he hated the school, and so he quit before the notice of expulsion. He enrolled in a polytechnic institute for his final two years of high school.

That summer, Susan White and Jack Bowden decided to get engaged, though their fears about whether it was a wise decision led them to postpone the actual marriage. However, they did sleep together now when the children were at home. When his mother told Jody about her engagement, he said, "I don't care." Susan wondered if Jody was jealous of the attention she gave Jack's son Christopher.

The polytechnic school had thousands of students instead of the hundreds at his private school, but Jody seemed to be doing well. In February, 1977, Jody crashed his sister's car while high on marihuana. During a confrontation with his mother, Jody told her he had been smoking it since May 1976. He said he needed it to feel better and to study. Susan asked him not to drive while high and to try to cut down on its use. Jody agreed. (In retrospect she wished she had forbidden him to use it and had sought counseling for him.)

Since his mother didn't get home till about 8:15 every night, Jody would come home to an empty house about four (O'Donnell was now at college as well), go to a friend's house to do his homework and arrive home after eight for his mother to fix dinner.

By April 1977, Jody's relationship with Lauren was causing him a lot of pain. In a race that month, Jody ran well but was weak because he hadn't raced since Christmas (when he broke his arm in the driveway after crashing into a friend's bike). He came in second in the first race but kept crashing in the second race. He seemed depressed at his performance, (Lauren had been there to watch him), and it turned out to be the last time he raced. Susan tried to get him to work on a fitness program to get his strength back, but he seemed uninterested.

On May 9th 1977, Susan got a telephone call while she was getting ready for the evening news program from Majorie who was at home. Jody had shot himself with a rifle in his bedroom. He left a suicide note saying it was because of Lauren, and later conversations with Lauren revealed that he had threatened to kill himself if she didn't go back with him. Just before he killed himself, he had called Lauren to tell her he was going to shoot himself and to say good-bye. (He had told some other friends a month earlier that he was going to kill himself because Lauren didn't love him - just as his father had.) Susan White found *The Little Prince* on the desk in his room, a book in which the hero commits suicide and whose author committed suicide soon after writing it.

Analysis

Jody's suicide seems remarkably like his father's. Both shot themselves in their bedrooms because the woman they loved had rejected them. Both killed themselves in such a way as to maximize the guilt in their loved ones. Jody's mother notes how similar her son's behavior in the face of Lauren's rejection was to that of her husband when he was trying to get her to marry him.

Jody certainly did not work through the feelings he had after his father's suicide. His mother notes that she was not used to communicating feelings and that she preferred to pretend things were fine. She calls herself a 'Susie Sunshine.' She says that she ought to have obtained grief counseling for the family and drug counseling for Jodie. She ought to have spent more time with Jody and communicated her love for him.

Jody eventually became close to his father. The similarities between his behavior and his father's shows that Jody identified strongly with him. His suicide was modeled closely upon his father's. Thus, the father seems to be the critical person influencing Jody's life. (It is noteworthy that, so far as we know, Jody's two sisters have not been suicidal and have not imitated their father's suicidal behavior.)

It is interesting to note that Jody does not appear to have been psychiatrically disturbed, and his drug use does not appear to have been extensive (as far as we know he used only marijuana). His problems with girl friends are typical of teenage dating life. His expulsion from school seems to have served his goals. Although his father was dead, Jody's close identification with him may have led to an internal need to excel in performance so that failure, (to win a bike race and perhaps even in academic pursuits), may have been particularly stressful for him. However, it was his relationship with Lauren that seems to have precipitated his suicide, but this stress may have been made harder to cope with given his poor performance in the bike racing. (We are not told how he was doing at his new school.)

So, in conclusion, the striking feature of Jody's suicide is the imitative aspect. What makes it unusual is that the imitation followed so soon upon the father's suicide. (Ernest Hemingway and John Berryman, for example, did not kill themselves until entering old age.)

◆ ◆ ◆

Substance Abusers

We have mentioned in Chapter 1 that drug abuse and alcoholism in themselves are considered by some investigators to be suicidal behaviors, *chronic suicide* to use the term suggested by Menninger (1938). Substance abusers are killing themselves, (shortening their lives and making them less fulfilling), because of their life style.

However, substance abusers are also often suicidal in more direct ways. Stenback and Blumenthal (1964) predicted that alcoholics should show less concern for their bodily integrity in general. They found that alcoholics attempted suicide more and had hypochondria less than other psychiatric patients. Most of the follow-up studies of alcoholics have reported higher rates of completed suicide than we would expect by chance. A comparison of alcoholics who kill themselves with those who died of the physiological consequences of the alcoholism found that the alcoholic suicides were more often psychiatrically disturbed, especially with affective disorders (Haberman, 1979).

Similarly, drug addicts have been found to have high rates of attempted suicide, 19 percent in a study by Saxon, et al. (1978), and high rates of completed suicide.

However, it is by no means clear why there is an association between substance abuse and suicide. It may be that certain predisposing factors, (physiological, childhood trauma, personality traits or the social milieu), lead to both a higher risk of substance abuse and of suicidal behavior. It may be that substance abuse increases the likelihood of suicidal tendencies. Or it may be the other way round, namely that suicidal tendencies increase the likelihood of substance abuse. No research has yet sought to test empirically whether any of these three possibilities have validity for particular groups of suicidal people.

Suicide in substance abusers often makes as little sense to us as suicide in adolescents because there do not appear to be sufficient causal elements in the circumstances leading up to the suicide. The substance abuse in itself is not a sufficient cause since most substance abusers do not commit suicide.

In the following case, that of the comedian Freddie Prinze who shot himself at the age of twenty-two, the substance abuse was quite extensive. He used valium, marihuana, cocaine and quaaludes. He had periods of deep depression and mania, as well as symptoms of schizophrenia, though the extent to which these symptoms were a result of the drug abuse is not clear.

CASE 12: Freddie Prinze

Freddie Prinze, a successful comedian, was only twenty-two when he shot himself. He had performed at the pre-inaugural ball for President Carter only ten days earlier. He was not someone who had been successful and who was now facing a decline. Rather he was a star on the way up. How did he come to kill himself?

The information used here to make some sense of his suicide is taken from the book by his mother, Maria Pruetzel (1978).

Parents and Childhood

Frederick Karl Pruetzel was born on June 22, 1954 in New York City. His mother, Maria, was an immigrant from Puerto Rico and his father, Karl, was Hungarian and an immigrant from Germany. (Karl emigrated in 1934 at the age of 19.) Karl, had been married before and had had three children. (Both Karl and his son Freddie were only children of second marriages and unusually close to their mothers.) During his first marriage, Karl was painting his house one day, and his five year old daughter drowned in the swimming pool. He was too late to save her, and he blamed himself for her death. He drank heavily, though the drinking did not affect his work. His second wife, Maria, felt that this experience reinforced his fear of taking responsibility for his son Freddie. Since Karl also worked nights, he spent little time with his son. Karl and Freddie did things together on weekends and holidays (such as horseback riding). However, Maria writes that she raised Freddie by herself. "Life was not easy for me, but I needed to be strong because Freddie needed me then...(p. xii)". Maria lived near her family, (her sisters even had an apartment in the same building, and her brother and then her father lived with her for a time), and so, all of the relatives helped take care of Freddie and shower him with love. Freddie was the only baby in the extended family, and there is the suggestion that Freddie was pampered.

Maria was younger than her husband. She was devoutly religious. When Freddie was ill in first grade, she prayed. As he lay dying from a gunshot wound, she prayed. Oral Roberts was the focus of her religious faith.

Freddie was also religious, though less so. He carried a bible with him and frequently asked his mother to pray for him. He had a fantasy of becoming a minister in a small town. (He had never lived in a small town!) Later, his mother-in-law was a devout Southern Baptist.

Childhood

Maria notes that Freddie had large numbers of relatives (though Maria mentions mainly the Puerto Rican relatives), but no one in the family was a child. Thus, Freddie had few peers to play with.

In first grade, Freddie became very ill, and his illness was initially misdiagnosed as tuberculosis. Later he was re-diagnosed as asthmatic, but the medications did not prevent visits to the emergency room. Eventually, a third doctor diagnosed the problem as an allergy to the medications that Freddie was being given and switched him to natural medicines. Freddie got well.

Initially, Freddie went to the public schools, and suffered from the bullying and extortion. He was fat as a child which may have facilitated him being a victim. He often cried over the stress of attending the school. Maria describes him as a misfit there, often alone, crying in his loneliness.

He took four years of piano lessons and then switched to the guitar. Maria bought him a guitar for $150 when he was fourteen, and he worked hard at learning it. (He sold one song for $200.) Interestingly, the pampering is evident in the circumstances surrounding the purchase of the guitar. His mother bought him it in exchange for him painting the apartment. He painted a little and then persuaded his mother to do the rest. She acquiesced.

Toward the end of his stay at the public school, he became the class clown. He skipped classes, and his academic grades declined. However, he lost his childhood pudginess, and he received school awards for his music and dramatic abilities (in June 1970).

In 1968, Freddie's uncle Mango (who was thirty six) was living with them and had just got engaged. He died unexpectedly, and Freddie took it hard. (He was fourteen years old.) Maria describes him as withdrawn and confused, and he cut school for a month. Three months later, Freddie's grandmother died in Puerto Rico, but his mother did not take him to the funeral there.

High School

After he graduated from junior high school, Maria took him to Puerto Rico for a holiday, and he was sociable and happy, dating girls and having fun. In the Fall, he was accepted at the High School of the Performing Arts in New York City.

Maria was anxious at her son becoming independent from her. Freddie persuaded Maria to give him seventy dollars a week so that he could take a taxi to school. He liked being driven in style to the school in front of the students and teachers. To get more money, he took an ushering job at a movie theater.

In the summer of 1971, he performed in musical shows for the Alliance of Latin Art. He also decided to join a rock band at the school. So he persuaded his mother to get him a job at her factory, where he worked hard and earned enough to buy some drums. (He paid half and, his mother paid half.) In the Fall of 1971, he joined the band as drummer.

(Maria frequently helped Freddie out with bills. For example, she found out in 1973 that Freddie owed a restaurant near his high school $1400. Maria paid it in three installments.)

In his second year at the school, he met his first love, Ann Sadlier. She was a year behind him. Freddie is described as being very domineering with her, yet generous. They broke up in January, 1973, when Freddie was eighteen, because Ann was upset by his flirting with other girls. Freddie tried to get her to change her mind many times in the next couple of years, but she refused, though they did remain friends. Ann also admitted that she was afraid of Freddie going into show business because then he would not have time for her.

Also in his second year, his friends suggested that he develop his comic skills, and so he began performing at the comedy clubs in the city. In the summer of 1972, he decided to quit the Alliance musical shows and the rock band, and to focus on comedy. (He still worked as an usher at the movie house.) He went from club to club, moving up in status as a comedian. Maria reports, though, that when his act did not go over well with the audience he would feel depressed, and he would appear to have been crying.

Academically, Freddie performed badly, failing English, history, economics and Spanish. However, he refused to go to summer school. He dropped out of school in 1973.

Career

In 1973, Freddie changed his name from Pruetzel to Prinze and began to focus on developing his career as a comic. His talent enabled him to move up to better clubs, and he acquired a manager, David Jonas. By July, 1973, Freddie was appearing at hotels and clubs

A two-week engagement in Puerto Rico did not go well. He was lonely and sent for his girl friend. The Puerto Ricans felt that his humor was insulting to them, though the vacationing hotel audiences liked him.

When he came back from Puerto Rico, he decided to move out from his parents' apartment, but after three days he moved back in with them.

By the end of 1973, Freddie was appearing on television shows (Jack Paar and eventually the Tonight Show). In 1974, he auditioned for and was given a part in *Chico And The Man* a television sitcom on NBC . He liked Los Angeles and decided to stay there, but he missed Ann, who still refused to be with him, and he described himself as lonely and depressed. He had developed the habit of using the telephone to keep in touch with people, running up bills of $800 a month. In his diary, he wrote that there was no one there to protect him. He called home nightly.

Success And Disintegration

While in Los Angeles, his producer, Jimmy Komack, found out that Freddie was using cocaine (in addition to valium and quaaludes). He sent him to a physician, Edward Ablon, who continued to prescribe him quaaludes until his suicide.

After *Chico And The Man* aired, it was a success, but Freddie got anonymous death threats. (Chicanos were upset that Freddie was depicting one of their ethnic group.)

In October, 1974, he fired his manager, David Jonas, who then filed a law suit against Freddie.

In December 1974, he sent his mother the fare to go to Puerto Rico and, in February 1975, the fare to come to Los Angeles. During that trip, Maria picked out the house that Freddie would buy for her and Karl.

In March 1975, while performing at Lake Tahoe, Freddie met Kathy Barber, a divorced woman, whom he eventually married. Kathy got pregnant in June, and they were married in October. His secretary Diane quit, and Maria concluded that Diane was romantically attached to Freddie and saw his marriage as a rejection. A friend of Kathy's became his secretary. During this time, Maria thought that Freddie was withdrawn and not as open to her as in the past. Freddie seemed to be drifting away from her.

Kathy went to a hypnotherapist, William Kroger, for help in natural childbirth, and Freddie began to see him to cure his drug addiction. In March 1976, Freddie's son, also called Freddie, was born. He said to his mother, "I don't have to feel lonely any more."

By April he was having problems with his marriage. Kathy did not like his drug abuse. There may have been other problems, but neither of them discussed it with Maria.

In November, Maria describes Freddie as distressed, depressed, confused, and exhausted. Also angry - he fired his gun recklessly at times and dislocated his wrist by hitting a wall with it. The legal battle with his manager continued, (his contract was upheld by the court for three years), and he separated from Kathy, who filed for divorce. He was arrested for driving while on drugs.

A Psychiatric Evaluation

He described his state as a nervous breakdown. In October 1976, Dr. Kroger gave Freddie the MMPI, and the computer report described Freddie as possibly schizophrenic. It concluded by saying that his responses suggested a major emotional disorder and recommended professional evaluation. His fantasies were almost delusional. He was suspicious and paranoid, avoided close interpersonal relationships and was unable to express his emotions in modulated ways. The report described him as disoriented, perplexed, hostile, negativistic and suspicious. He was described as sensitive to criticism, ready to blame others, and likely to misinterpret the actions of others.

Interestingly, the report described him as alienated from his family and perceived little love in his home. He found home life unpleasant. This is in contrast with the picture presented by his mother.

The report also described him as excitable, volatile, full of energy, high-strung and unpredictable.

The End

During December and January, Freddie's condition worsened. At various times, his producer, Jimmy Komack, and his hypnotherapist, William Kroger, removed his drugs and his gun. Each time he demanded them back. His secretary describes him as sinking deeper into depression. Off quaaludes he was manic; on them he was depressed.

His weight had dropped from 204 pounds to 165 pounds, and he had diarrhea. He told his father he was bleeding internally. On January 19, 1977, Freddie performed at the pre-inaugural ball for President Jimmy Carter. On the way back, he stopped for a break at Las Vegas and obtained more quaaludes.

During the final few days, his friends kept visiting him, and he kept calling them. He received the divorce agreement from Kathy's lawyers. During the early hours of January 29th, matters came to a head. He called Kathy at 12:15 am on the 29th, (her birthday), and spoke to her for a few minutes. His secretary was there, and at 1:15 am Dr. Kroger arrived. Carol left. Dr. Kroger left. He called his financial manager, Dusty Snyder, who went to be with Freddie. Freddie shot himself in the head in front of Dusty. Thirty-three hours later he was declared dead.

Analysis

Freddie Prinze was addicted to drugs. He took valium, marihuana, cocaine and quaaludes. He tried to end his drug abuse, in particular, by visiting a hypnotherapist, but with how much motivation we do not know. Apart from his drug abuse, he appears to have had virtually no criminal involvement outside of traffic violations. (For example, he was in trouble for driving without a license when he was sixteen and for driving under the influence of drugs prior to his suicide.) Maria gives us little idea of how Freddie got into drugs or when his drug abuse escalated.

Freddie seems to have had many friends once he got to high school. And thereafter he had many acquaintances, girl friends and friends. Yet he appears to have been lonely much of the time. This suggests two things. First, perhaps his social relationships were superficial and not gratifying? He may fit the hysterical personality (or pattern of vicarious living as described by Andras Angyal).

In the pattern of vicarious living, the child grows up unliked for himself. Therefore, he assumes a personality that he thinks will get him approval, and he suppresses his real personality. Once this tactic has been adopted, the person needs continual attention and approval from others to support his assumed personality. It also leads to feelings of emptiness because of the suppression of the real self.

This makes sense given Freddie's eventual desire for entertaining audiences and his upset when they didn't like his act. The audiences rewarded his act, and his friends were necessary for supporting his personal style.

Since Freddie's mother seems to have loved and liked him, what is the source of Freddie's problems with self-esteem? The answer must lie in his father, the father who feared responsibility for his child, who worked nights, and who is the missing figure in the biography by Maria. It is interesting that his MMPI profile was that of someone who was alienated from his family, in contrast to the impression given by Maria.

Maria describes Freddie as quite domineering. His requests sounded like orders. When he wanted money, he had no qualms about taking it from her without telling her. However, he never denied taking it. Interestingly, in his brief life, he paid her back, as he promised he would, by sending her money for trips and buying her a house in California. Although self-centered, he does not appear to have been selfish, and in fact he was quite generous.

His love relationships were failures. The first woman he loved left him because of his flirting (and possibly because of his domineering ways). His marriage was a brief affair, lasting only a year and a half from the first meeting of the couple to the filing for divorce. His wife mentioned the drug abuse as a problem, but Freddie's interpersonal style probably contributed to the disintegration of the marriage.

Freddie's mother appears to have pampered Freddie. He was her only child. She sees herself as having raised him by herself and at personal cost. She allowed him to have whatever he wanted and bailed him out of difficulties. She also seems to have bound Freddie to her, a bond that Freddie himself seems to have had difficulty breaking. As her child, he functioned adequately. Away from her, he disintegrated.

An overweight child, rejected by his peers, chooses a career that will win him the adulation of audiences, alienates those whom he loves and who might love him, and becomes a drug addict.

In the last few weeks of his life, the stress increases. His manager wins a law suit against him, his wife files for an expensive divorce, his drug addiction remains uncured, and his success as a comedian is always only as good as the last audience. He sees himself as having a nervous breakdown.

As he comes to the decision to kill himself, which as far as we can tell from his mother's biography was not a long-standing preoccupation, his religious beliefs were not strong enough to deter him and the methods for suicide were close at hand, a gun and pills. He shot himself in front of his financial manager, which suggests anger. However, nothing in the biography explains the anger that Freddie might have felt, unless it was rooted in anger felt toward his rejecting father.

CHAPTER 7

PREVENTING SUICIDE

In this chapter we will consider whether we ought to prevent suicide and, if we decide that under certain conditions the answer is yes, how we can prevent suicide.

To consider these issues in the abstract is easy but often irrelevant to the lives of real people. For example, we will discuss the possibility of restricting people's access to lethal means for committing suicide. The research is fine, and the arguments quite convincing. However, is it really possible to restrict a particular individual from access to the means for suicide?

So let us first present a case of suicide with which most of us are familiar, Ernest Hemingway. Hemingway has long fascinated Americans and continues to do so. Articles and biographies about him appear regularly, and so we are familiar with many of the details of his life. After we have read his case, then we will turn to an examination of the ethics and methods of suicide prevention and explore whether any of the proposals makes sense for Ernest Hemingway. Could he have been prevented from killing himself?

CASE 13: Ernest Hemingway

Ernest Hemingway was born in Oak Park, a suburb near Chicago, on July 21, 1899. Both of Ernest's grandfathers served in the Civil War, and Anson Hemingway in particular was always relating heroic tales of the war. Ernest grew up reading military histories, and was fascinated by the recent wars: the Spanish-American War of 1898, the Boer War in 1899-1902, and the Russo-Japanese War in 1904-1905. In his later life, Ernest went to five wars, in Italy, Turkey, Spain, China and France.

He was raised in a town that was white, Protestant, prosperous and conservative. The family was very religious, with morning family prayers and Bible reading and church on Sundays. The Sabbath was strictly enforced, and after punishment the children had to kneel down and ask God for forgiveness. Later, Hemingway moved far from those values, even eventually converting to Catholicism but their influence stayed with him.

Ernest's mother, Grace, was a talented contralto, and gave up a potential career in music, supposedly, because the stage lights hurt her eyes and because she married Ed. She gave music lessons, earning a fair amount of money.

Ernest's father, Ed, was a doctor, specializing in obstetrics. He seems to have been dominated by his wife. For example, he promised at the time of their marriage that she would never have to do housework. He kept his word, cooking, shopping, doing the laundry and supervising the servants. Grace seemed pampered, spoiled and selfish. In many ways, Ernest learned to never relate to his wives the way his father had related to his wife. Although Grace and Ed got on each other's nerves, they were happy with each other and in love. They had six children, and Ernest was the second-born and first-born son.

Ernest's Childhood

Ernest's childhood was relatively uneventful. Other siblings were born, he went through school and graduated, he played sports, took music lessons with his mother, and learned to hunt and fish with his father.

For three years, he was dressed in girl's clothing and had his hair long, so that he would look like a twin to his elder sister, Marcelline. Meyers (1985) dismisses this since it was often the custom to do this to boys in Victorian times. But Meyers misses the point that there are often events that are common to all or most of us, but that does not preclude their having special relevance to some of us.

Ernest's later life can be seen as the epitome of the macho masculine life style. This exaggerated style makes his early years of cross-gender identity of interest. Not only this, but Ernest had periodic episodes of impotence: when he first left Hadley, (his first wife), for Pauline, (his second), during his infatuation with Jane Mason in 1936, in 1944 in Paris when he was courting Mary, (his fourth wife), and in 1960 during his depression.

In addition, Ernest was constantly fascinated by the merging of identities between a man and his lover. In several novels, the lovers resemble each other physically and switch roles. In *The Garden of Eden*, Catherine wants to be a man and calls David Catherine, while David wants to be a woman and calls Catherine Pete. Ernest, himself, reversed names when he wrote to a young woman he was in love with in his old age, Adriana Ivancich. Latham (1977) suggests that Ernest experimented with sex role reversal with his wives, and Mary, (his fourth wife), records an imaginary interview in which Ernest says he likes sodomy and that his wife is a boy. Meyers also suggests that Ernest had a hair fetish (though he documents only a literary preoccupation with hair).

Meyers certainly documents Ernest's exaggeration of his sexual conquests and sexual performance, while his wives if they commented at all tended to criticize his performance. Finally, Ernest often showed a pronounced hostility to homosexuals. All of this certainly points to some sexual conflict within Ernest.

Portents of his Later Life-Style

Early on, his mother noted Ernest's tendency to be aggressive, self-confident, and courageous and to exaggerate. Meyers records adolescent fights with his parents, for example, over eating vegetables, wanting to wear long trousers at the age of fifteen, working on the family farm in the summer, and playing the cello in the family orchestra. His cruelty to animals is first shown at the age of six when he hacked a porcupine to pieces.

At school, he was competitive, developed an interest in boxing and began to write. He rejected the idea of going to college and instead went to work for the *Kansas City Star*. However, the war appealed to him, and he volunteered as a Red Cross ambulance driver and left for Italy in 1918, at the age of 18.

Just before leaving the United States, he announced his engagement to a film star whom in fact he had never met. His parents believed him and were upset. This develops a theme in his life which had always been present, but eventually grew to pathological proportions. Ernest could not tell the truth about himself. He exaggerated, invented, and distorted his version of his life. In his version, he stopped being an ambulance driver in the First World War and became a soldier and leader. He boasts of sexual conquests that never existed, such as his "African wife" and of "irrigating" Mary four times in a night, when he was probably impotent. He changes his version of his life after significant events, imputing motives and actions to his relatives and wives which are false. For example, he blamed his mother for his failure to go to college, (since she spent the money for the tuition on her houses), whereas in fact he chose not to go.

This is a fascinating trait, especially since we find it in Marilyn Monroe, who also committed suicide. It is as if Ernest did not like himself and could not accept that others would like him. He had to invent a person whom he thought people would like and surround himself with cronies who would like the person he invented. He shows the typical neurotic pattern described by Carl Rogers. Rogers felt that if children were not liked for themselves and that if conditions of worth were set up for them by their parents, then they would suppress their true selves and develop a false social self that was designed to win approval from others.

In this regard, it is interesting to note that his parents, and especially his mother, disliked his intention to write fiction and in fact threw him out in 1920. They were horrified by his published works and considered them disgusting and obscene. They were also morally offended by his divorce from his first wife and by his conversion to Catholicism. It is fascinating to read Ernest's letters to his parents in which he tries to explain his writing and justify it. He is still, as an adult, trying to get his parents to like and approve of him.

The First World War

Ernest's experiences in the war provided two critical events. First, he was injured. On July 18, 1918, a shell landed three feet from him, while he was handing out chocolate to soldiers in the trenches. It killed a man standing between him and the shell, and he received over 200 shell fragments. Some of these, (perhaps ten), caused quite severe wounds, and there have always been rumors of damage to his genitals. Again Meyers minimizes the importance of this event. However, others, such as Young (1966), noted that Ernest was passive in this first confrontation with death, and he spent the rest of his life and his fiction facing death and actively challenging it. He went to wars and sometimes fought in them, he faced bulls in Pamplona, he shot big game, and in the end he caused his own death. It is as if he had a repetition compulsion, to relive that panic that he felt in his first experience with death and this time prove himself to himself.

Meyers quotes Ernest writing about Mussolini: ".....all his martial bombast and desire for military glory was a defense mechanism, formed against his own knowledge of how frightened he had been in the world war and the ignominious exit he had made from it....." (Meyers, 1985, p. 96). This seems so apt for Ernest himself. Peter Wykeham said that Ernest impressed him as ".....the sort of man who spends his whole life proving that he is not scared."

Although at first, during his convalescence in Italy, he seemed to have few symptoms of trauma, after he had returned to the United States and home, he suffered from insomnia and could not bear to have the lights out. To help him, his sister Ursula, (who was three years younger than him), used to sleep with him at night. It is likely that the war experience was very traumatic for Ernest.

The second major event of the war was that he fell in love with a nurse, Agnes von Kurowsky. What made the experience traumatic was that, after he had gone back to the United States, believing that they were in love and would marry, she wrote to him and rejected him for another. This was Ernest's first real love, and we might note that he was still a virgin, and it led him to never trust women again. In each marriage, he was looking for the next partner should the current wife reject him, and he perhaps cast them off before they could cast him off. The situation is more complex, of course, since as each wife got to know him better, it would have been harder for him to maintain the false self that he created to deal with his feelings of worthlessness. It would have been harder to deceive his wives about the real Hemingway.

His Marriages

His first marriage was to Hadley Richardson in 1920, a woman eight years older than Ernest. This marriage came only one year after his first sexual experience, which was with a waitress. Hadley had some similarities to Ernest's mother, having also tried but abandoned a career in music. She was submissive, adopted his interests, (in boxing, fishing and drinking), and tried to keep him as her husband. Meyers denies that she was a mother substitute, despite the appropriateness of the role for her. However, she used to sign her letters to Ernest as "Mummy." She clearly helped Ernest work out problems he had experienced with his mother, and he managed to create a role for himself very different from his father's role with his wife. They had one son, John.

Meyers notes, however, that perhaps Gertrude Stein served as a mother substitute for Ernest, resembling Ernest's mother in age, talent, egocentricity, and anger with and rejection of Ernest when he succeeded.

After an infatuation with Duff Twysden in 1925, Ernest fell in love with and married Pauline Pfeiffer in 1927. She was four years older than Ernest. They had two sons, Patrick in 1928 and Gregory in 1931. In 1932 he became infatuated and had an affair with Jane Mason. This ended in 1936, and Ernest met Martha Gellhorn later that year. She was nine years younger than Ernest. They married in 1940 and had the least satisfactory marital relationship of the four marriages. Martha was away a good deal of the time, working as a journalist, and when they were together they fought violently and abusively. Martha was less submissive than the previous two wives and less willing to put up with Ernest's behavior, which was getting worse as he got older.

He met Mary Welsh in 1944 and was married to her from 1946 until his death in 1961. Mary, like Martha, was nine years his junior. He still wanted a daughter, but Mary had a tubular pregnancy which left her sterile. During his marriage to Mary, Ernest had two flirtations, with Nancy Hawks and Virginia Viertel, and two infatuations with young women, Adriana Ivancich and Valerie Danby-Smith. Meyers does not think that Ernest ever slept with either of his last loves.

Meyers notes that as Ernest aged, his wives and loves became younger and younger. In his youth he married older women, and in his old age he fell in love with young women. However, this is not an unusual pattern for men.

Relations with his Family

Ernest ended up on bad terms with most of his family. He called his father a coward for his suicide, hated his mother and blamed her for his father's death and much more, quarreled with his elder sister Marcelline and his younger sister Sunny, rejected another younger sister (Carol) for her marriage, reacting much like an Oedipal father in his jealousy of her husband, rejected his young brother Leicester despite Leicester's attempts to emulate and flatter Ernest, criticized his son Jack and quarreled with Gregory. Only Ursula, (the one who slept with him during his recovery after the First World War), remained in favor up till the end.

With his sons, he seems to have ignored them as babies (as did Pauline, the mother of the youngest two). Later he seems to have been more devoted to them, but their adolescence brought attempts to dominate them and adulthood brought sexual rivalry (according to Meyers), especially as Ernest's wives and romantic figures became younger. His will left nothing to his sons.

Relations with Friends

In the 1920s, in Paris, Ernest was friendly with other authors and artists. However, by 1937 he had quarreled with almost all of these friends. He found reason to attack each of them, especially if they showed any disapproval of his writing or his behaviors. His attacks could be in print and physical. Charles Sweeny described him as extraverted, suspicious, unloyal and violent. He seemed especially scared if people got too close to him.

Meyers characterizes him as a swaggering hero in the 1930s, a drunken braggart in the 1940s, and a sad wreck in the 1950s. Ernest replaced his intellectual friends in the 1930s with soldiers, sportsmen, millionaires, hangers-on and sycophants. (With such people, drinking and engaging in sports, one can be friendly but safely distanced.) He also seemed to need a few people around him with whom he could be a domineering father/teacher. Meyers sums up Ernest's needs for friends. He needed and liked to have around him father-mentor figures, soldier-heroes, kid brothers, surrogate sons, trusty drivers and erotic teenage females.

Yet clearly Ernest had attractive traits. He could be generous and entertaining, and he was brave. In a psychological analysis, it is too easy to focus on what is pathological and to neglect that which is healthy.

Literary Criticism

Ernest has been considered one of the finest writers in America in the Twentieth Century. He received the Pulitzer Prize in 1952 and the Nobel Prize in 1954. However, Ernest was always wounded by negative reviews, of which he received many. They made him feel undervalued and were severe blows to his confidence. They reinforced his doubts about his creativity, talent and future productivity. He usually reacted with anger at his critics, and he sought to attack them in retaliation.

This pattern fits in with our analysis of Ernest as someone who was never liked for himself as a child and who never came to like himself. When critics attacked him, fairly or unfairly, he lacked the inner sources of self-esteem to enable him withstand their attacks.

Alcoholism and Depression

As Hemingway aged, his drinking began to resemble alcoholism more and more. He was already drinking brandy in large quantities when he was in the hospital recovering from his wounds in the First World War. By the 1930s he is reported to have been drinking up to seventeen scotch and sodas a day. His drinking increased in the 1940s, when he was drinking continuously. Eventually, the alcohol consumption caused physiological damage, and these problems exacerbated his physical decline in the later 1950s.

Interestingly, most of his friends (and enemies) thought he could hold his alcohol well. He rarely passed out and did not appear to have developed some of the side-effects of alcoholism, such as dt's, blackouts or nutritional deficiencies. He seems to have developed the French pattern of being steadily intoxicated rather than the American pattern of binge drinking.

He is reputed to have had regular periods of depression throughout his life, though Meyers does not emphasize this at all. In the 1940s, Ernest usually woke up happy, but could not maintain this mood for the whole day. His depression was especially strong if he did not drink. He called his depressions his "black-ass" moods. Meyers notes that there is no evidence that Ernest ever had a manic phase. At the end of his life, he was suffering from severe depression and was given ECT by doctors at the Mayo Clinic in a fruitless effort to ameliorate it.

Other interesting symptoms apparent during his life included obsessive traits, manifested in his counting of the words he wrote, the animals he killed and, later on, daily recording of his blood pressure and weight. He began to show excessive anxiety in the early 1940s, especially about taxes and his financial solvency. With regard to the myths he created about himself, Meyers notes that it seemed as if Ernest came to act as if the myths were true.

Ernest almost never accepted any responsibility for events, preferring to externalize the blame. For example, he blamed his mother for his unhappy childhood (part of the myth he created) and for preventing him going to college, he blamed Pauline and Dos Passos for breaking up his marriage to Hadley, Jinny Pfeiffer for breaking up his marriage to Pauline, and Gregory (his son) for causing Pauline's death. Gregory attributed this trait to his father's remorseful conscience. But it seems more likely to be the result of his dislike of himself. To have accepted the blame would probably have increased his sense of worthlessness and depression and made suicide more likely.

Ernest's fascination with killing is also of interest here. He learned to hunt and fish with his father. His experienced his first fighting in Italy during the First World War, and then moved on to a fascination with bull fighting. He pursued his interest in hunting, followed later wars and eventually got to kill men (German soldiers) during the Second World War.

Why did he kill? Hotchner (1966) quotes Ernest as saying, "I spend a hell of a lot of time killing animals and fish so I won't kill myself." Thus, Ernest, himself, saw his killing as a way of externalizing his anger, which fits the classic psychoanalytic theory of depression and suicide.

Mental Illness in his Family

Ernest's father showed symptoms of suspiciousness and paranoia at the end of his life. He was depressed and completed suicide. Two of Ernest's sons had episodes of mental illness. Patrick became paranoid schizophrenic in 1947 and received electroconvulsive therapy, which destroyed his memory. Later, in 1957, Gregory who had often abused drugs, had a mental breakdown and also received electroconvulsive therapy.

Thus, there is evidence of psychiatric illness in three generations of Hemingways. Believers in the medical model of psychiatric illness would see this as suggesting genetically-caused psychiatric illness in the family. However, the existence of disturbed family systems provide an equally plausible explanation of three generations of psychiatrically ill people. Crazy people not only pass on their genes, they provide an unhealthy atmosphere in which their children are raised.

Suicide in Ernest's Social Network

Suicide abounded in Ernest's social network. We have already mentioned the attempted suicide of his maternal grandfather and the suicide of his father, of course. The father of his first wife, Hadley, killed himself in 1903. His lover Jane Mason attempted suicide in 1933 by jumping, breaking her back but surviving. One of his servants killed herself in the 1950s, and one of his biographers (Charles Fenton) jumped to his death. In 1983, twenty-two years after Ernest's suicide, one of his later loves, Adriana Ivancich hung herself.

After his father's suicide, Ernest said that he would probably die in the same way, and he began to consider suicide much more often. He asked for the gun his father used, and then threw it in a lake, as if to prevent himself using it. Perhaps his rejection of his father's act was also a means of convincing himself not to die the same way.

Accidents and Illnesses

Meyers presents an incredible list of accidents and illnesses that Ernest experienced. He had many concussions, shot himself accidentally, and suffered severe burns, cuts, fractures, and internal injuries.

Meyers notes that the likelihood of accidents was increased by Ernest's bad temper, recklessness, irritability, bad vision, slow reflexes, clumsiness and heavy drinking. However, the fact the Ernest would box others, both bare fisted and with gloves, run with the bulls in Spain, shoot big game, and follow wars placed him in the position to get hurt. He is, in Shneidman's (1968) terminology, a death-chancer and death-hastener, and Menninger (1938) would see Ernest's behavior as a manifestation of his self-destructive impulses.

To dispel any notion that Ernest's accidents were simply bad luck and that self-destructive motives played no role, one can note that after a severe concussion in London in 1944, when it was recommended that his head be opened and the hemorrhage drained, he left the hospital and went on a bombing flight with the RAF instead, risking severe brain damage.

Final Stresses

Toward the end of his life, Ernest experienced the loss through death of many of his friends. His publishers, Max Perkins and Charles Scribner died, as did Pauline, (his second wife), his mother, and his childhood friend Katie Dos Passos. In the last year of his life, he was upset by the deaths of Gary Cooper and George Vanderbilt.

In 1954, he was in Africa on a safari, and he survived two plane crashes in the space of a few days. He received very serious injuries, and this time his body seemed not to recover. The actual crash injuries included liver and kidney damage, burns and impaired vision and hearing. But more importantly, he lost confidence, and friends described him as an "old man."

After the crashes, he was believed to have died, and so he was able to read his obituaries. For those who contemplate suicide, the fantasy of how one will be viewed after death is fascinating. Ernest got to experience this before his real death, and perhaps he was pleased by this preview of how he would be viewed.

The Final Months and the Mayo Clinic

In late 1960, Ernest began to deteriorate rapidly. He was depressed and his obsessions continued. He developed pathological fears about taxes that he might owe and other unlikely infringements of the laws. He develop a paranoid fear of persecution from a variety of sources. He accused a driver of trying to kill him, Mary of trying to get rid of him in the Mayo clinic and, in particular, of the FBI. (His paranoid accusations against the FBI had a basis in reality since they had kept a file on him since his days in Cuba, even talking to his doctor at the Mayo Clinic. As Meyers notes, even paranoids have real enemies.) He became unable to make decisions, over matters such as which clothes to wear or which motel to stay in.

His physical condition was serious. He had a chronic skin disease, eye problems, hypertension, diabetes, and liver and kidney disease. In addition, his hair loss and impotence upset his image of himself. Hotchner (1966) quotes Ernest as saying that "if I can't exist on my own terms, then existence is impossible."

He was admitted to the Mayo Clinic in December 1960, released in January 1961, readmitted in April 1961 and released in June 1961. During the first admission he received eleven to fifteen ECTs and ten more in his second admission. There was no change in his symptoms. However, the ECT did damage his memory. At home between the two admissions, he was unable to write even a few sentences, and he complained about his loss of memory. He was convinced that there was no cure for his psychiatric problems.

Meyers is strong in his criticism of the Mayo Clinic. He sees Ernest's treatment as worsening his life situation, deepening his depression and destroying his memory. He castigates the doctors for releasing him rather than transferring him to a different institution. He particularly focuses on the use of ECT, and notes that Ernest had never attempted suicide until after his first release from the Mayo Clinic. Indeed, Ernest made several suicide attempts during the trip to readmit him to the Mayo Clinic in April 1961, trying to walk into the propellers of an airplane and trying to jump from the airplane. Valid though Meyers criticisms are, he is writing in 1986 when our knowledge about ECT is more complete and when there are powerful anti-depressant medications available. Ernest's treatment was not unusual in 1960.

Despite these reservations about patient care at the Mayo Clinic, it would not have been surprising if Ernest had killed himself even had he never been admitted to the Mayo Clinic or any other psychiatric institution. The sources and causes of Ernest's suicide lay far beyond the treatment received at the Mayo Clinic.

Ernest and Suicide

Ernest had thought of suicide all his life. From his reading *The Suicide Club* by Stevenson as an adolescent, to his thoughts of suicide during marital crises, Ernest had always seen suicide as a way to die. He predicted that he would kill himself with a gun, and in the 1930s told others that a shotgun in the mouth was the way to complete suicide. He said that he had often talked himself out of it, but he saw suicide as solution to a painful and humiliating death from a serious illness. He saw suicide as a way of going out in a blaze of light at one's peak rather than as a deteriorated wreck.

Meyers views his eventual suicide as motivated by desperation at his physical and psychological deterioration, with elements of self-pity and revenge, (against Mary whom he left to find his disfigured head when she came down). Meyers also hints at elements of psychic homicide, since though Mary locked up Ernest's guns she left the keys out for him to find. Perhaps his suicide was a welcome relief for her?

Analysis

The presence of psychiatric illness in several generations of the Hemingway family suggests the role of genetic factors in predisposing members of the family to depression. But let us assume that there was indeed a genetic predisposition to depression, and therefore suicide, in the Hemingway family. The timing of the suicides shows the influence of learning. Not all patients who are depressed kill themselves in old age when suffering from a severe illness. Many kill themselves long before this stage.

Ernest, like his father, killed himself only when he was suffering from diabetes and other physical illnesses and when under other stress (financial reversals for his father; a creative block for Ernest). Both used guns, and both killed themselves when others were around. Ed Hemingway killed himself while his thirteen year-old son was at home; Ernest while his wife Mary was at home. This suggests that, for both of them, anger at the rest of the family was a component of the suicidal action.

From his mother, Ernest learned that she really wanted a daughter, and this affected him for the rest of his sexual life. He suffered from impotence and sought to establish a macho image that could not be mistaken for sex-role confusion. From his father, he learned not to let women dominate him the way his mother dominated his father.

From his parents, he learned that he was not very likable. Thus, he learned not to reveal himself, and he began to build up a social self that would hide the real Ernest and present a mask to others that would get their admiration and approval. This distortion of the truth about himself became almost pathological in its extent. This led to him casting off friends before they could really hurt him and to difficulties in coping with reviews of his literary work.

From Agnes he learned that women could not be trusted and that you had better have a replacement ready in case your wife deserted you. From the First World War, he learned that he was scared by death so that he needed to prove to himself that he could face death without fear, again and again and again.

Ernest was exposed to suicide from a young age. He was six when his grandfather tried to shoot himself. He was twenty-nine when his father shot himself. In adulthood, many of his friends and acquaintances attempted or committed suicide. And he talked about it continuously. To take just one example, Flanner (1972) talked with Ernest in 1944 and agreed with him that liberty could be as important in the act of dying as in the act of living. They promised not to grieve if the other committed suicide. After his father's suicide, though he condemned his father for cowardice, he said that he would probably die in the same way.

The experience of reading his obituaries showed Ernest that he would be appreciated and lauded after his death. Thus, suicide would achieve escape from pain and help establish him in people's memory in the way that he desired.

Ernest knew quite clearly that he displaced his self-destructive impulses by killing animals. He felt that if he stopped killing animals, he might kill himself.

Finally, Ernest's suicide secured for him an escape from tremendous physical and psychological pain. It was the best alternative for him, given the circumstances into which he had got himself by the time of his old age.

In some ways it seems foolish to ask why Ernest killed himself because it seems like the ideal way for him to die. He lived life to the full - loving attractive women, drinking, fighting, and hunting. He had won universal acclaim as a writer. But now he was sixty and unable to continue this style of living. He was diseased, impotent, depressed and no longer able to write. It would be hard for us to imagine Ernest dying as a frail old man, locked up in a mental hospital, trying to convince others of the validity of his paranoid delusions.

Yet that is what makes Ernest's death interesting. Because other men move gracefully into old age and assume roles that befit them. They can become at peace with themselves and the world and serve as models for us. Or they can become sources of wisdom that we turn to for their views on life and the world. But Ernest could not fill these roles.

In a sense, Ernest killed himself many years before his death, when he began to suppress his true self, build up a phony image of himself and surround himself with cronies who would reinforce this phony image. As Ernest got older, his true self became more and more deeply buried, and his phony image more and more pathological. Until at the end, Ernest was the antithesis of the psychologically healthy person.

◆ ◆ ◆

Should We Prevent Suicide?

Before we consider the efforts that have been made to prevent suicide, we should address the issue of whether we should prevent suicide. All of us have to die, and so the issue is not whether to die but how to die. Few of us give any consideration to the manner of our death until we are dying and it is too late to affect the dying process. But take some time now.

Do you want to die in a car accident with your body crushed and mangled, from cancer after a long and debilitating illness, or alone in a home for the poor? Most of us say that we want to die peacefully in our sleep, but that will happen to few of us.

Lester (1970) has discussed the concept of what is an *appropriate* death. Included in the criteria were the timing of death, (is death occurring at the appropriate time in your life), the quality of your life, (is your life of sufficient quality to make continued living worth while), and the possibility of playing a role in your own death.

When we look at Ernest Hemingway, we can see that at the time of his death, the quality of Hemingway's life was very poor. His physical health was deteriorating, and he was suffering from a severe psychiatric disturbance. He could look forward to continued physical and mental problems with long-term hospitalization.

In addition, he was no longer able to live the style of life to which he had become accustomed, the macho life style involving women, fighting and drinking for which he was well-known. He was suffering from a writer's block made worse by the memory loss resulting from the electroconvulsive therapy he had received.

Hemingway had little to look forward to, save for a few declining years. The timing was appropriate for his death. In addition, Hemingway's life was characterized by activity. After the passive confrontation with death in the First World War, Hemingway continually confronted and challenged death. It was consistent for him to face this last challenge as actively as he had all of the previous challenges. Death was not an event that should steal up on Hemingway and take him unawares and against his will. Hemingway should have confronted death and taken it into his own hands.

So, perhaps, Hemingway ought to have killed himself in that way he did at the time he chose? As did Percy Bridgman (1882-1961) who was dying from Paget's disease. There was no cure, and Bridgman was in great pain. He was rapidly losing mobility, whereupon he took his own life. His suicide note read:

> *It isn't decent for society to make a man do this thing himself.*
> *Probably this is the last day I will be able to do it myself.*
> *P.W.B. (Kemble, et al., 1970).*

This view, however, is not without its opponents. Shneidman (1966) set his goal as that of preventing everyone from killing himself. Pretzel (1968) argued that no suicide can be rational, and Robins, et al. (1969) argued that virtually all suicides are psychiatrically ill. The view of suicidal states as temporary crises also leads to the conclusion that we should prevent suicide since the crisis will soon pass (Tabachnick, 1970). Battin and Maris (1983) have recently edited a collection of articles on this and related issues.

Of course, when a person requests help during a crisis, the situation is quite different. If the person voluntarily asks for assistance, we are morally bound to respond (Lester, 1981).

How to Prevent Suicide

Traditionally, preventive efforts have been classified into three main types. In *primary* prevention we try to prevent the development of suicidal tendencies in the society and in the individual. This is, of course, the most difficult kind of prevention for psychological problems. It presupposes that we know the causes of suicide, which we do not. Furthermore, changing society so as to make it different may simply create different psychological problems. For example, Henry and Short (1954) have seen depressed/suicidal behaviors as opposed to assaultive/murderous behaviors. Changes in the society which would make suicide less common may well make murder more common!

How might primary prevention have helped Hemingway? Hemingway's relationship with his mother was not wonderful. It would be unfair to categorize it as bad, since it is not hard to find mother-son relationships that are much worse. Nonetheless, perhaps some form of family counseling could have improved the family atmosphere? Hemingway's father committed suicide. If we could have prevented that act, perhaps suicide would not have become the exit of choice for the Hemingway family? Perhaps the father should have received counseling?

Hemingway was a risk-taker, but we really cannot forbid car racing, parachute jumping, and all other death-defying activities. Ernest's first episode of impotence was after his adultery during his first marriage. Can we prevent adultery and the break up of marriages? In old age, Hemingway's ability to write disappeared, his physical strength deserted him, and his pleasures diminished. Old age is, however, inevitable.

And even had we put the whole Hemingway family in individual and family counseling, there is no evidence that Hemingway's suicide would have been averted. After all, we can easily find cases of suicide in those who have been in counseling.

Secondary Prevention

Secondary prevention is the early intervention with people who are on the verge of killing themselves. There are several strategies that have been tried here.

Suicide Prevention Centers

Suicide prevention centers have become increasingly common in the last few decades (Lester and Brockopp, 1973; Zusman and Davidson, 1971). The core treatment modality for a suicide prevention center is a 24-hour telephone counseling service. People in distress can call in at any time and speak to a counselor. Most of these services are staffed by volunteers who are paraprofessionals. This means that they have limited counseling skills and rarely have any professional or graduate-level counseling skills. As a result, there has been a great deal of criticism of the adequacy of these services (McColskey, 1973).

Standards have been proposed for suicide prevention centers (Motto, 1969), and at the present time the *American Association of Suicidology* certifies and re-certifies suicide prevention centers to ensure that standards are maintained.

Occasional suicide prevention centers have walk-in clinics for face-to-face counseling, store fronts in skid row sections of cities, counseling teams that can go to where the distressed client is, (telephone counselors are typically forbidden to leave the center or to have face-to-face constant with clients), and follow-up of those who have attempted suicide or had a relative commit suicide.

Do these suicide prevention centers prevent suicide? Initially, the answer was negative. Despite an early report (Bagley, 1968) that suicide prevention centers in Great Britain (where they are all run by the Samaritan organization), later research failed to show a preventive effect (Barraclough, et al., 1977). Similarly, in the USA, early research found that cities with suicide prevention centers and those without centers all experienced a rising suicide rate in the 1960s and early 1970s (Lester, 1974).

However, a more recent study of counties in the USA showed that the presence of a suicide prevention center did appear to have an impact on the suicide rate of white females (Miller, et al., 1984). Since white females are the most common client group calling suicide prevention centers (Lester and Brockopp, 1973), this result makes good sense. However, no report of a replication study has yet appeared, and so we must be cautious in our conclusions.

The American approach to the apparent failure of suicide prevention centers to prevent suicide was to focus on ways in which they could be improved (Resnick and Hathorne, 1973). For example, the importance of identifying high risk groups in the population and fashioning programs specifically for them was stressed. However, Auerbach and Kilmann (1977) criticized using suicide rates as a measure of the effectiveness of suicide prevention centers. Such centers may provide excellent crisis intervention and act as the central information and referral agency for all of the psychological resources in the community. Auberbach and Kilmann argued that evaluation should focus on measures of changes in client behavior rather than a simple "Did he die" criterion.

Removing the Means for Suicide

A growing idea in the suicide prevention movement has been that, if we were to make the means for killing oneself less readily available, we may lower the suicide rate. Anecdotally, it has long been noted that suicidal people are often sent home to a home that contains more than enough material for committing suicide (Robin and Freeman-Browne, 1968). Barraclough, et al. (1971) reported a number of cases such as the following.

> *A 45-year old, single woman lived alone since the recent death of both parents. She was drawing sick benefits on psychiatric grounds but was actively looking for work. In the preceding seven years there had been four admissions for agitated depression, with reasonable response to treatment. At the time of death her drug treatment was amitryptyline 100 mg daily and Sodium Amytal 1G (15 gr.) daily. This prescribing was recorded for the previous six months but had probably been going on for 12 months. She had not seen the doctor for seven months and obtained prescriptions on request from his receptionist. There had been a recent recurrence of her depressive symptoms. (Barraclough, et al., 1971, p. 652).*

Cases have been recorded where patients have forged prescriptions in order to obtain lethal drugs (Friedman, 1966), and the physician and pharmacist should work closely to prevent suicidal people obtaining supplies of lethal drugs.

Several research studies have been conducted to document the effect of restricting methods for suicide.

(1) Detoxifying Domestic Gas

In England and Wales, the detoxification of domestic gas, in which coal gas with a high carbon monoxide content was eventually replaced by natural gas, was accompanied by the virtual elimination of suicide by domestic gas and a one-third reduction in the overall suicide rate (Kreitman, 1976). However, the detoxification of domestic gas in Scotland and the Netherlands was not accompanied by an overall reduction in the suicide rate, though Clarke and Mayhew (1989) have argued that this was because the suicide rate in those countries was rising at the time of detoxification.

(2) Gun Availability

Lester (1984) conducted a series of studies to show that states with stricter handgun control laws in the USA had lower firearm suicide rates and lower suicide rates overall. This research has been supplemented by evidence that actual rates of gun ownership were similarly related to a reduced firearm suicide rate (Lester, 1987c) and by a time-series study (Clarke and Jones, 1989) that showed that years in which more households had handguns also had higher firearm suicide rates and higher overall suicide rates.

(3) Motor Vehicle Exhaust

In the USA since 1968, emission controls have been imposed on cars. The result has been that the carbon monoxide content of car exhaust has been drastically reduced, so that it is much harder to commit suicide using car exhaust and failed attempts are becoming more common (Hay and Bornstein, 1984). Clarke and Lester (1987) documented how the percentage of suicides in the USA using car exhaust has dropped since the imposition of emission controls. However, the percentage of suicides using car exhaust is quite small, about nine percent in 1968, so that no impact from emission controls on the overall suicide rate was detected.

The major question that has been raised about these data is whether those who are prevented from using their preferred method for suicide because it is unavailable would switch to an alternative method. Lester's (1984) data on the effect of strict handgun control laws suggested that restriction of handguns reduces the overall suicide rate, so that switching does not appear to take place. However, in Great Britain, where there are no emission controls on cars, there has recently been a dramatic increase in the use of cars for suicide (Clarke and Lester, 1987). This suggests that those who would have used domestic gas for suicide have slowly come to realize that car exhaust may be used instead. As this information is getting disseminated in the society, the use of car exhaust is increasing, leading to a higher rate of suicide in Great Britain. This issue promises to be a major research topic in the next decade.

Would restricting the availability of methods for suicide have prevented Hemingway from killing himself? Mary Hemingway locked up his guns the night before his death, but left the keys hanging on their regular hook. In the morning, Hemingway unlocked the gun cabinet and used a gun to kill himself. What would he have done had the guns been removed from the house?

Hemingway had made other suicide attempts, such as walking into the propellers of a plane and trying to jump from the plane. However, such methods are not as likely to be lethal, since others are around and can prevent the suicide (as in fact they did in Hemingway's case). Thus, even if we only switch people from one method to another, we may be able to switch them to methods less likely to result in death and thus prevent their death.

More recently, Lester (1988d) has argued that suicidologists should take social and political action on this issue. For example, they should join the fight to restrict gun sales and prescriptions, and they should initiate law suits to force the society to restrict access to methods for suicide. For example, it has been shown that people drive over other bridges in the San Francisco in order to jump from the Golden Gate Bridge (Seiden and Spence, 1983-1984). Since the local government has failed to fence in the Golden Gate Bridge even though they know that people will use it for suicide, perhaps law suits brought by the relatives of suicides would force the local government to fence in the bridge, just as homeowners in the USA are required to fence in their backyard swimming pools.

Effective Treatment and Clinics

The provision of adequate psychological and psychiatric services could be seen as a useful way of preventing suicide, though there is no good research to show that the provision of general mental health facilities does prevent suicide (Lester, 1987c).

However, increasing attention is being given to the accurate diagnosis of depression (which is the most common psychiatric state accompanying suicidal preoccupation) and the prescription of appropriate medication. For example, Barraclough (1972) has argued that accurate diagnosis of bipolar affective disorder (manic-depressive psychosis) and prescription of lithium would prevent a great number of suicides.

In addition, recent research has investigated which medications are most effective in preventing suicide (Montgomery and Montgomery, 1984) and which psychotherapies have proven to be most effective (Liberman and Eckman, 1981).

Ernest Hemingway was hospitalized in the 1960s when treatment, both by medication and by psychotherapy, was not as effective as today. It may well be that current treatment techniques would have alleviated Hemingway's depression and paranoia and prolonged his life. However, patients in treatment today still commit suicide, and the American suicide rate has not changed much in the last twenty years. It is, therefore, hard to place much confidence in the effectiveness of treatment.

Tertiary Prevention

Tertiary prevention involves the prevention of the recurrence of suicide in those who have already been suicidal. The techniques for tertiary prevention are identical to those for secondary prevention, except they are directed toward the chronically suicidal rather than the first-time suicidal person.

Discussion

Diggory (undated) has taken a much more optimistic view of suicide prevention than many suicidologists. He argued that the improving medical emergency services prevent large number of suicides. In 1971 in Pittsburgh, for example, he estimated that the suicide rate was reduced from 15.2 per 100,000 per year to 12.5 simply by saving the lives of those who had attempted suicide. And emergency medical care has improved since then. In addition, Diggory argued, immediate psychiatric treatment and referrals to appropriate community agencies also saves lives. Diggory estimated that overall thirty-four percent of suicidal deaths are prevented.

What may prove difficult is to prevent additional suicides!

BIOGRAPHICAL SOURCES

Bell, Q. *Virginia Woolf.* New York: Harcourt Brace Jovanovich, 1972.
Berkow, I., & Olderman, M. An American tragedy. In J. Thorn (Ed.) *The armchair book of baseball.* New York: Scribners, 1985, 46-66.
Flanner, J. *Paris was yesterday.* New York: Viking, 1972.
Frank, G. *Judy.* New York: Harper & Row, 1975.
Gallant, M. *The affair of Gabrielle Russier.* New York: Knopf, 1971.
Hotchner, A. *Papa Hemingway.* New York: Bantam, 1966.
Guiles, F. L. *Legend.* Stein & Day, 1984.
Hemingway, L. *My brother, Ernest Hemingway.* Cleveland: World, 1961.
Keats, J. *You might as well live.* New York: Simon & Schuster, 1970.
Koestler, A. *The case of the midwife toad.* New York: Random House, 1971.
Lahr, J. *Prick up your ears.* New York: Knopf, 1978.
Latham, A. A farewell to machismo. *New York Times Magazine*, 1977, October 16, 52-99.
Meyers, J. *Hemingway.* New York: Harper & Row, 1985.
Pruetzel, M. *The Freddie Prinze story.* Kalamazoo: Master's Press, 1978.
Stokes, H. S. *The life and death of Yukio Mishima.* New York: Farrar, Straus & Giroux, 1974.
White-Bowden, S. *Everything to live for.* New York: Poseidon, 1985.
Young, P. *Ernest Hemingway,.* New York: Harcourt, Brace & World, 1966.

REFERENCES

Angyal, A. *Neurosis and treatment.* New York: Wiley, 1965.
Anon. *Juvenile suicides in adult jails.* Urbana: University of Illinois, 1983.
Asinof, E. *Two lives for peace.* New York: Viking, 1971.
Auerbach, S., & Kilmann, P. Crisis intervention. *Psychological Bulletin,* 1977, 84, 1189-1217.
Bakwin, H. Suicide in children and adolescents. *Journal of Pediatrics*, 1957, 50, 749-769.
Baechler, J. *Suicides.* New York: Basic, 1979.
Bagley, C. The evaluation of a suicide prevention scheme by an ecological method. *Social Science & Medicine*, 1968, 2, 1-14.
Bagley, C., Jacobson, S., & Rehin, A. Completed suicide. *Psychological Medicine*, 1976, 6, 429-438.
Barraclough, B. M. Suicide prevention, recurrent affective disorder and lithium. *British Journal of Psychiatry,* 1972, 121, 391-392.
Barraclough, B. M., Jennings, C., & Moss, J. R. Suicide prevention by the Samaritans. *Lancet,* 1977, 1, 237-239.
Barraclough, B. M., Nelson, B., Bunch, J., & Sainsbury, P. Suicide and barbiturate prescribing. *Journal of the Royal College of General Practitioners*, 1971, 21, 645-653.
Barraclough, B. M., & Shepherd, D. Birthday blues. *Acta Psychiatrica Scandinavica*, 1976, 54, 146-149.

Battin, M., & Maris, R. *Suicide and ethics.* New York: Human Sciences Press, 1983.

Beck, A. T., Kovacs, M., & Weissman, A. Hopelessness and suicidal behavior. *Journal of the American Medical Association,* 1975, 234, 1146-1149.

Beck, A. T., & Lester, D. Components of suicidal intent in completed and attempted suicide. *Journal of Psychology,* 1976, 92, 35-38.

Bock, E., & Webber, I. Suicide among the elderly. *Journal of Marriage and the Family,* 1972a, 34, 24-31.

Bock, E., & Webber, I. Social status and relational system of elderly suicides. *Life-Threatening Behavior,* 1972b, 2, 145-159.

Breault, K. D. Suicide in America. *American Journal of Sociology,* 1986, 92, 628-656.

Clarke, R. V., & Jones, P. R. Suicide and the increased availability of handguns. *Social Science & Medicine,* 1989, 28, 805-809.

Clarke, R. V., & Lester, D. Toxicity of car exhausts and opportunity for suicide. *Journal of Epidemiology & Community Health,* 1987, 41, 114-120.

Clarke, R. V., & Mayhew, P. Crime as opportunity. *British Journal of Criminology,* 1989, 29, 35-46.

Conte, H., & Plutchik, R. Personality and background characteristics of suicidal mental patients. *Journal of Psychiatric Research,* 1974, 10, 181-188.

Corder, B., Page, P., & Corder, R. Parental history, family communication, and interaction patterns in adolescent suicide. *Family Therapy,* 1974, 1, 285-290.

Cumming, E. Lazer, C., & Chisholm, L. Suicide as an index of role strain among employed and not-employed married women in British Columbia. *Canadian Review of Sociology & Anthropology,* 1975, 12, 462-470.

Danigelis, N., & Pope, W. Durkheim's theory of suicide as applied to the family. *Social Forces,* 1979, 57, 1081-1106.

Diggory, J. D. Empirical evidence for the improved prevention of suicide. Undated.

Douglas, J. *The social meanings of suicide.* Princeton: Princeton University Press, 1967.

Dublin, L. I. *Suicide.* New York: Ronald, 1963.

Durkheim, E. *Suicide.* New York: Free Press, 1951.

Ellis, A. *Humanistic psychotherapy.* New York: Julian, 1973.

Farberow, N. L. *The many faces of suicide.* New York: McGraw-Hill, 1980.

Farberow, N. L., & Shneidman, E. S. *The cry for help.* McGraw-Hill, 1961.

Frank, M. L. & Lester, D., Temporal variation of suicide in teens and young adults. *Perceptial and Motor Skills,* 1988, 67, 586.

Friedman, G. Suicide and the altered prescription. *New York State Medical Journal,* 1966, 66, 3005-3007.

Galbraith, J. K. *The great crash 1929.* Boston: Houghton-Mifflin, 1954.

Glueck, S., & Glueck, E. *Unraveling juvenile delinquency.* New York: Commonwealth Fund, 1950.

Goldstein, K. *Human nature in the light of psychopathology.* Cambridge: Harvard University Press, 1940.

Gottesman, I., & Shields, J. Schizophrenia in twins. *British Journal of Psychiatry,* 1966, 112, 809-818.

Gove, W. Sex, marital status and suicide. *Journal of Health & Social Behavior,* 1972, 13, 204-213.

Green, A. Self-destruction in battered children. *American Journal of Psychiatry,* 1978, 135, 579-582.
Greene, J. W., & Keown, M. Depression and suicide in children and adolescents. *Comprehensive Therapy*, 1986, 12(2), 38-43.
Haberman, P. Cause of death in alcoholics. *Proceedings of the 10th International Congress on Suicide Prevention.* Ottawa: IASP: 1979, 108-115.
Harris, R. A. Factors related to continued suicidal behavior in dyadic relationships. *Nursing Research,* 1966, 15, 72-75.
Hattem, J. V. Precipitating role of discordant interpersonal relationships in suicidal behavior. *Dissertation Abstracts*, 1964, 25, 1335-1336.
Hay, P., & Bornstein, R. Failed suicide attempt by emission gas poisoning. *American Journal of Psychiatry* 1984, 141, 592-593.
Hendin, H. *Suicide and Scandinavia.* New York: Doubleday, 1964.
Hendin, H. *Black suicide.* New York: Basic, 1969.
Henry, A. F., & Short, J. F. *Suicide and homicide.* New York: Free Press, 1954.
Heston, L. Psychiatric disorder in foster-home reared children of schizophrenic mothers. *British Journal of Psychiatry*, 1966, 112, 819-825.
Hlady, W. G., & Middaugh, J. P. The under recording of suicides in state and national records, Alaska, 1983-1984. *Suicide & Life-Threatening Behavior,* 1988, 18, 237-243.
Hoskin, J. O., Friedman, M., & Cawte, J. A high incidence of suicide in a preliterate society. *Psychiatry,* 1969, 32, 200-210.
Humphrey, J., Niswander, D., & Casey, T. A comparison of suicide thinkers and attempters. *Diseases of the Nervous System*, 1971, 32, 825-830.
Jacobs, J. A phenomenological study of suicide notes. *Social Problems,* 1967, 15, 60-72.
Jacobs, J. *Adolescent suicide.* New York: Wiley, 1971.
Johnson, B. D. Durkheim's one cause of suicide. *American Sociological Review,* 1965, 30, 875-886.
Kallman, F. *Heredity in health and mental disease.* New York: Norton, 1953.
Kemble, E., Birch, F., & Holton, G. Bridgman, Percy Williams. In C. Gillispie (Ed.) *Dictionary of scientific biography.* New York: Scribners, 1970, 2, 457-461.
Korrella, K. Teenage suicidal gestures. *Dissertation Abstracts International,* 1972, 32A, 5039.
Kramer, M., Pollack, E., Redlick, R., & Locke, B. *Mental disorders/suicide.* Cambridge: Harvard University Press, 1972.
Kreitman, N. The coal gas story. *British Journal of Preventive & Social Medicine,* 30: 86-93, 1976.
Kreitman, N., Smith, P., & Tan, E. Attempted suicide in social networks. *British Journal of Preventive & Social Medicine*, 1969, 23, 116-123.
Kumler, F. R. Communication between suicide attemptors and significant others. *Nursing Research,* 1964, 13, 268-270.
Labovitz, S., & Hagedorn, R. An analysis of suicide rates among occupational categories. *Sociological Inquiry,* 1971, 41, 67-72.
Leenaars, A. *Suicide notes.* New York: Human Sciences, 1988.
Leonard, C. V. *Understanding and preventing suicide.* Springfield: Thomas, 1967.
Lester, D. Attempted suicide as a hostile act. *Journal of Psychology*, 1968, 68, 243-248.
Lester, D. Suicidal behavior in men and women. *Mental Hygiene,* 1969, 53, 340-345.

Lester, D. Resentment and dependency in the suicidal individual. *Journal of General Psychology,* 1969a, 81, 137-145.

Lester, D. The concept of an appropriate death. *Psychology,* 1970, 7(4), 61-66.

Lester, D. Suicide and homicide in open and closed societies. *Psychological Reports,* 1971, 29, 430.

Lester, D. *Why people kill themselves.* 1st Edition. Springfield: Thomas, 1972.

Lester, D. Effect of suicide prevention centers on suicide rates in the United States. *Health Services Reports,* 1974, 89, 37-39.

Lester, D. Suicide in police officers. *Police Chief,* 1978, 45(4), 17.

Lester, D. Temporal variation in suicide and homicide. *American Journal of Epidemiology,* 1979, 109, 517-520.

Lester, D. The morality of counseling the suicidal person. *Journal of Counseling & Psychotherapy,* 1981, 4(1), 78-84.

Lester, D. *Why people kill themselves.* 2nd Edition. Springfield: Thomas, 1983.

Lester, D. *Gun control.* Springfield: Thomas, 1984.

Lester, D. Suicide in Communist Europe. *Psychological Reports,* 1984a, 54, 628.

Lester, D. Genetics, twin studies and suicide. *Suicide & Life-Threatening Behavior,* 1986, 16, 275-285.

Lester, D. The birthday blues revisited. *Acta Psychiatrica Scandinavica,* 1986a, 73, 322-323.

Lester, D. Suicide, homicide and the quality of life. *Suicide & Life-Threatening Behavior,* 1986b, 16, 389-392.

Lester, D. *The death penalty.* Springfield: Thomas, 1987.

Lester, D. *Suicide as a learned behavior.* Springfield: Thomas, 1987a.

Lester, D. Suicide and sibling position. *Individual Psychology,* 1987b, 43, 390-395.

Lester, D. Preventing suicide. In J. Morgan (Ed.) *Suicide: helping those at risk.* London, Ont.: King's College, 1987c, 69-78.

Lester, D. Availability of guns and the likelihood of suicide. *Sociology & Social Research,* 1987d, 71, 287-288.

Lester, D. Murder and suicide: are they polar opposites? *Behavioral Sciences & the Law,* 1987e, 5, 49-60.

Lester, D. The stability of national suicide rates in Europe, 1875-1975. *Sociology & Social Research,* 1987f, 71, 208.

Lester, D. Benefits of marriage for reducing risk of violent death from suicide and homicide for white and nonwhite persons. *Psychological Reports,* 1987g, 61, 198.

Lester, D. Religiosity and personal violence. *Journal of Social Psychology,* 1987h, 127, 685-686.

Lester, D. A subcultural theory of teenage suicide. *Adolescence,* 1987h, 22, 317-320.

Lester, D. *The biochemical basis for suicide.* Springfield: Thomas, 1988a.

Lester, D. *Why women kill themselves.* Springfield: Thomas, 1988b.

Lester, D. Sex differences in the fear of different consequences of death. *Perceptual & Motor Skills,* 1988c, 66, 550.

Lester, D. Suicide prevention. *AAS Newslink,* 1988d, 14(2), 8.

Lester, D. What does the study of simulated suicide notes tell us? *Psychological Reports,* 1988e, 62, 962.

Lester, D. One theory of teenage suicide. *Journal of School Health,* 1988f, 58, 193-194.

Lester, D. Personal violence (suicide and homicide) in South Africa. *Acta Psychiatrica Scandinavica,* 1988g, 1989, 79, 235-237.

Lester, D. Youth suicide: a cross-cultural perspective. *Adolescence*, 1988g, 23, 955-958.

Lester, D., & Beck, A. T. Early loss as a possible sensitizer to later loss in attempted suicides. *Psychological Reports*, 1974, 39, 121-122.

Lester, D., Beck, A. T., & Mitchell, B. Extrapolation from attempted suicides to completed suicides. *Journal of Abnormal Psychology*, 1979, 88, 78-80.

Lester, D., & Brockopp, G. W. *Crisis intervention and counseling by telephone.* Springfield: Thomas, 1973.

Lester, D., & Frank, M. Sex differences in the seasonal distribution of suicide. *British Journal of Psychiatry,* 1988, 153, 115-117.

Lester, D., & Perdue, W. C. The detection of attempted suicides and murderers using the Rorschach. *Journal of Psychiatric Research*, 1974, 10, 101-103.

Liberman, R., & Eckman, T. Behavior therapy versus insight-oriented therapy for repeated suicide attempters. *Archives of General Psychiatry*, 1981, 38, 1126-1130.

Linehan, M. Suicide and attempted suicide. *Perceptual & Motor Skills*, 1973, 37, 31-34.

Litman, R. E. Sigmund Freud on suicide. *Psychoanalytic Forum*, 1966, 1, 206-214.

MacMahon, B., Johnson, S., & Pugh, T. Relation of suicide rates to social conditions. *Public Health Reports*, 1963, 78, 285-293.

Maris, R. *Social forces in urban suicide.* Homewood: Dorsey, 1969.

Maris, R. The adolescent suicide problem. *Suicide & Life-Threatening Behavior,* 1985, 15, 91-109.

Masumura, W. T. Social integration and suicide. *Behavior Science Research,* 1977, 12, 251-269.

McColskey, A. S. The use of the professional in telephone counseling. In D. Lester & G. W. Brockopp (Eds.) *Crisis intervention and counseling by telephone.* Springfield: Thomas, 1973, 238-251.

Menninger, K. *Man against himself.* New York: Harcourt, Brace & World, 1938.

Miller, H., Coombs, D., Leeper, J., & Barton, S. An analysis of the effects of suicide prevention facilities on suicide rates in the US. *American Journal of Public Health,* 1984, 74, 340-343.

Montgomery, S., & Montgomery, D. The prevention of suicide acts in high-risk patients. *Advances in Biochemical Psychopharmacology*, 1984, 39, 315-317.

Motto, J. Development of standards for suicide prevention centers. *Bulletin of Suicidology*, 1969, March: 33-37.

Myers, D., & Neal, C. Suicide in psychiatric patients. *British Journal of Psychiatry,* 1978, 133, 38-44.

Neuringer, C. The thinking processes in suicidal women. In D. Lester (Ed.) *Why women kill themselves*. Springfield: Thomas, 1988, 43-52.

Nurnberger, J. I., & Gershon, E. S. Genetics. In E. S. Paykel (Ed.) *Handbook of affective disorders.* New York: Guilford, 1982, 126-145.

Ogden, M., Spector, M., & Hill, C. Suicides and homicides among Indians. *Public Health Reports,* 1970, 85, 75-80.

Palmer, S. *A study of murder.* New York: Crowell, 1960.

Paykel, E. Life stress. In L. Hankoff & B. Einsidler (Eds.) *Suicide.* Littleton, MA: PSG, 1979, 225-234.

Peck, M., & Schrut, A. Suicidal behavior among college students. *HSMHA Health Reports,* 1971, 86, 149-156.

Pfeffer, C., Conte, H., Plutchik, R., & Jerret, I. Suicidal behavior in latency age children. *Journal of the American Academy of Child Psychiatry,* 1979, 18, 679-692.

Philip, A. E. Personality characteristics of attempted suicides in Edinburgh. *Proceedings of the 5th International Congress for Suicide Prevention.* Vienna: IASP, 1970, 114-116.

Phillips, D. P. A review of the incidence of parental absence upon suicidal behavior. *Proceedings of the 10th International Congress for Suicide Prevention.* Ottawa: IASP, 1979, 50-53.

Phillips, D. The influence of suggestion on suicide. *American Sociological Review,* 1974, 39, 340-354.

Platt, S. Unemployment and suicidal behavior. *Social Science & Medicine,* 1984, 19, 93-115.

Platt, S. Parasuicide and unemployment. *British Journal of Psychiatry,* 1986, 149, 401-405.

Pokorny, A. D. Suicide and weather. *Archives of Environmental Health,* 1966, 13, 255-256.

Pretzel, P. W. Philosophical and ethical considerations of suicide prevention. *Bulletin of Suicidology,* 1968, July, 30-38.

Price, J. The genetics of depressive behavior. In A. Coppen & A. Walk (Eds.) *Recent developments in affective disorders.* British Journal of Psychiatry, Special Publication, Number 2, 1968, 37-54.

Quinney, R. Suicide, homicide and economic development. *Social Forces,* 1965, 43, 401-408.

Resnick, H. L. P., & Hathorne, B. *Suicide prevention in the 70s.* Rockville: NIMH, 1973.

Rich, C., & Pitts, F. Suicide by male physicians during a five-year period. *American Journal of Psychiatry,* 1979, 136, 1089-1090.

Richman, J. *Family therapy for suicidal people.* New York: Springer, 1986.

Robin, A., & Freeman-Browne, D. Drugs left at home by psychiatric patients. *British Medical Journal,* 1968, 3, 424-425.

Robins, E. *The final months.* New York: Oxford University Press, 1981.

Robins, E. Psychosis and suicide. *Biological Psychiatry,* 1986, 21, 665-672.

Robins, E., Murphy, G., Wilkinson, R., Gassner, S., & Kayes, J. Some clinical considerations in the prevention of suicide based on a study of 134 successful suicides. *American Journal of Public Health,* 1959, 49, 888-899.

Robins, E., & O'Neal, P. Culture and mental disorder. *Human Organization,* 1958, 16(4), 7-11.

Rojcewicz, S. War and suicide. *Life-Threatening Behavior,* 1971, 1, 46-54.

Rootman, I. A cross-cultural note on Durkheim's theory of suicide. *Life-Threatening Behavior,* 1973, 3, 83-94.

Rose, K., & Rosnow, I. Physicians who kill themselves. *Archives of General Psychiatry,* 1973, 29, 800-805.

Rosenbaum, M., & Richman, J. Suicide. *American Journal of Psychiatry,* 1970, 126, 1652-1655.

Rosenberg, M. L., Smith, J. C., Davidson, L., & Conn, J. M. The emergence of youth suicide. *Annual Reviews of Public Health,* 1987, 8, 417-440.
Ross, M. Suicide among physicians. *Diseases of the Nervous System,* 1973, 34, 145-150.
Roth, W. F., & Luton, F. H. The mental health program in Tennessee. *American Journal of Psychiatry,* 1943, 99, 662-675.
Rudestam, K. E. Survivors of suicide. In D. Lester (Ed.) *Suicide: the state of the art.* Philadelphia: Charles Press, 1989. 203-213.
Sainsbury, P., & Barraclough, B. Differences between suicide rates. *Nature,* 1968, 220, 1252.
Saxon, S., Kuncel, E., & Aldrich, S. Drug abuse and suicide. *American Journal of Drug & Alcohol Abuse,* 1978, 5, 485-495.
Schaefer, H. H. Can a mouse commit suicide? In E. S. Shneidman (Ed.) *Essays in self-destruction.* New York: Science House, 1967, 494-509.
Schulsinger, F. Kety, S., Rosenthal, D., & Wender, P. A family study of suicide. In M. Schou & E. Stromgren (Eds.) *Origin, prevention and treatment of affective disorders.* New York: Academic, 1979, 277-287.
Seiden, R., & Spence, N. A tale of two bridges. *Omega,* 1983-1984, 3, 201-209.
Shneidman, E. S. State programs in suicide prevention. Conference of the Surgeon General with State and Territorial Mental Health Authorities, 1966.
Shneidman, E. S. Orientation toward cessation. *Journal of Forensic Sciences,* 1968, 13, 33-45.
Shneidman, E. S., & Farberow, N. L. The logic of suicide. In E. S. Shneidman & N. L. Farberow (Eds.) *Clues to suicide.* New York: McGraw-Hill, 1957a, 31-40.
Shneidman, E. S., & Farberow, N. L. *Clues to suicide.* New York: McGraw-Hill, 1957b.
Shneidman, E. S., & Faberow, N. L. Statistical comparisons between committed and attempted suicides. In N. L. Farberow & E. S. Shneidman (Eds.) *The cry for help.* New York: McGaw-Hill, 1961, 19-47.
Shore, J. H., Bopp, J. F., Dawes, J. W., & Waller, T. R. A suicide prevention center on an Indian reservation. *American Journal of Psychiatry,* 1972, 128, 76-81.
Slater, E. A review of earlier evidence on genetic factors in schizophrenia. In D. Rosenthal & S. Kety (Eds.) *The transmission of schizophrenia.* London: Pergamon, 1968, 15-26.
Sletten, I., Brown, M., Evenson, R., & Altman, H. Suicide in mental hospital patients. *Diseases of the Nervous System,* 1972, 33, 328-334.
Spiegel, D., & Neuringer, C. Role of dread in suicidal behavior. *Journal of Abnormal & Social Psychology,* 1963, 66, 507-511.
Stack, S. Suicide. *Social Forces,* 1978, 57, 644-653.
Stack, S. Durkheim's theory of fatalistic suicide. *Journal of Social Psychology,* 1979, 107, 161-168.
Stack, S. Celebrities and suicide. *American Sociological Review,* 1987, 52, 401-412.
Stein, M., Levy, M., & Glasberg, M. Separations in black and white suicide attempters. *Archives of General Psychiatry,* 1974, 31, 815-821.
Stenback, A., & Blumenthal, M. Relationship of alcoholism, hypochondria, and attempted suicide. *Acta Psychiatrica Scandinavica,* 1964, 40, 133-140.
Stephens, B. J. The social relationships of women. In D. Lester (Ed.) *Why women kill themselves.* Springfield: Thomas, 1988, 73-85.

Stewart, A., & Winter, D. The nature and causes of female suppression. *Signs,* 1977, 2, 531-553.

Tabachnick, N. The crisis treatment of suicide. *California Medicine,* 1970, 112 (June), 1-8.

Tabachnick, N. *Accident or suicide.* Springfield: Thomas, 1973.

Temoche, A., Pugh, T. F., & MacMahon, B. Suicide rates among current and former mental institution patients. *Journal of Nervous & Mental Disease,* 1964, 138, 124-130.

US Public Health Service. *Promoting health/Preventing Disease: Objectives for the nation.* Washington, DC: US Government Printing Office, 1980.

van Winkle, N. W., & May, P. A. Native American Suicide in New Mexico, 1957-1979. *Human Organization,* 1986, 45, 296-309.

Vessey, M., McPherson, K., Lawless, M., & Yeates, D. Oral contraception and serious psychiatric illness. *British Journal of Psychiatry,* 1985, 146, 45-49.

Wechsler, H. Community growth, depressive disorders and suicide. *American Journal of Sociology,* 1961, 67, 9-16.

Wilson, P. T. A study of twins with special reference to heredity as a factor determining differences in environment. *Human Biology,* 1931, 6, 324-354.

Wolfgang, M. E. *Patterns of criminal homicide.* Philadelphia: University of Pennsylvania Press, 1958.

Zusman, J., & Davidson, D. L. *Organizing the community to prevent suicide.* Springfield: Thomas, 1971.

Subject Index

Punishment Experiences, 55-56